THE SECRETS OF MILLHAVEN

Will Beaudry

The Secrets of Millhaven

Paperback edition ISBN: 979-8-9900258-1-3

Hard Cover edition ISBN: 979-8-9900258-2-0

Ebook edition ISBN: 979-8-9900258-0-6

First Edition 2024

Book Cover Art by David Colón

Edited by Heidi Bechard, Midnight Edit LLC

In memory of DKC III

1

Wednesday, September 19, 1990

Clutching the black travel bag tighter, Erica rose from the bench and crossed the terminal toward the ladies' room. As she stepped off the blue carpet and passed over the threshold onto the equally blue-tiled floor, she couldn't help but notice how refreshingly different the air was. She could almost taste the flowery scent from the automatic freshener.

A chill ran through her as she set the bag on the counter, pushed a strand of brown hair to the side, and examined the days-old bruise under her right eye. The swelling was finally going away, and she noticed that the makeup she'd applied yesterday was wearing off.

She fished a small bottle of Ibuprofen from the bag, popped a handful into her mouth - she didn't bother counting them - then collected a handful of water and washed them down.

Leaning over the sink, she splashed another handful of water against her face.

There was movement behind her.

"Excuse me, sir; this is the ladies' room!"

She looked past her reflection to see a well-dressed African American man brush past a young, blonde woman, both of whom were entering the restroom.

How the hell did he find me?

She swiped her bag from the counter and swung it toward his head. He reached up and deflected the blow, grabbed the strap, and tugged, pulling her closer. She could smell his breath.

He grinned.

"What the hell?" The blonde woman yelled. She grabbed his arm and tried to pull him away, but he swatted her to the side with little effort. Erica brought her knee up and planted it between his legs.

He dropped to the floor, forcing his grip on her bag to loosen just enough for her to pull free.

Her eyes locked onto the woman's hands, where she saw a small can of pepper spray.

He, too, saw the can, and he lashed out and grabbed the woman's wrist. Erica heard a loud "crack," followed by an equally loud scream as he grabbed a clump of blonde hair and slammed the woman's head onto the countertop.

Erica kicked out again. Her foot connected with the side of his left knee, causing him to fall back to the floor.

She saw a small revolver as he pulled it from beneath his jacket. She shot a glance at her would-be savior, lying motionless on the tiled floor, scooped up her bag, and ran.

As she pushed her way through the crowd of newly arrived passengers, she motioned toward the restroom behind her. "He's got a gun!"

The terminal was suddenly alive with shouting as everyone headed toward the nearest exit, and two transit police officers rushed past her.

As she shoved her way through a set of glass doors and found herself in the bus loading area, it took a few seconds for her eyes to adjust to the dimly lit parking lot. She ducked between the two nearest buses, ran up the steps of the next one, and dropped into an empty seat toward the back.

She peered through the window as the doors closed and the bus lurched forward.

Her heart raced as adrenaline rushed through her veins. She could feel it in her already throbbing head.

As the bus pulled away, she was afforded a better view of the large windows and everyone who was still inside the terminal.

Jack stood with his back to her, waving his arms at the two transit cops.

A gold police shield bounced against his chest as he flipped a silver chain over his head.

Jesus, that was close.

She cradled the bag in her lap and laid her head on it.

Wait.

She didn't recognize the bag. It was the wrong size, the wrong color. In her rush to get away, she must have grabbed the other woman's bag by mistake.

Erica's I.D., money, and credit cards were all gone.

Her hands shook as she unzipped the bag and rummaged through the clothes. They were larger than hers, but she could make them work. She pulled the wallet out and unsnapped a magnetic flap. Inside, she found $300 in various denominations, a Colorado driver's license, and two credit cards.

She removed the license and read the name printed on it.

"Melissa Harmon."

She closed her eyes and recalled the look on the young woman's face as she ran from the restroom.

"I'm so sorry."

2

Kyle Lorne pulled his police cruiser into a spot just outside the TV repair shop. Usually, he'd park in front of the diner, but today was different. Today was the day he would give Lauren her gift, and he wanted to give himself time to work up the courage. It would take at least five minutes to get there if he used the crosswalk at the far corner.

Plenty of time to talk myself out of it.

He grabbed the briefcase off the seat next to him, climbed out, and took his time as he strolled past the bookstore, the Fudge Shoppe, and the flower store, all opening for the day. Across the street, next to the diner, several people were waiting in line at the bakery. A large blue neon sign was flashing FRESH DONUTS.

"Good morning, deputy."

He almost bumped into Alice as she emerged from the door to Alice's Treasures. It was the local go-to place for anyone looking for antiques. Most of the things she sold came from estate sales in and around Millhaven.

"Good morning, Alice."

"Bit cold out this morning, isn't it?"

"Just a bit. Could be worse."

"Could be worse," she agreed.

He reached the corner and waited for the little white icon to appear on the crosswalk signal. He scanned through the large storefront window across the street. Like it was every morning, the diner was crowded.

I don't see her. Maybe she's not working today.

The signal informed him that it was okay to cross. He looked up and

4

down the road several times, hoping a car would drive by, further barring him from his destination. He was a little disappointed that the street was devoid of traffic.

As he stepped off the curb and into the crosswalk, a waitress crossed in front of the door inside the diner.

Is that her?

He saw that it wasn't. It took a few breaths for his heartbeat to return to normal.

Don't be a wuss. Just go in there, order breakfast like you always do, and casually give it to her.

What if she doesn't like it?

She'll like it.

But what if she doesn't?

He grabbed the half-circle handle, took a deep breath, and pulled the door open. He paused as he took in the smell of fresh coffee and bacon before making his way to his usual booth, the one farthest from the door. From there, he would have a clear view of everyone inside.

He sat his briefcase on the table, popped open the latches, then removed a blue folder and set it next to the case.

I can do this.

He closed the lid and placed the case on the bench next to him, listening to the conversations going on around him.

Bea and Dorthea were discussing which housewife was cheating on whom; Andy was explaining to his son, Ben, the finer points of carburetors and how they were superior to fuel injectors. Ben was listening intently. At fifteen, he and his dad had been working on a father/son project for the last year, restoring an old '68 Chevy Chevelle.

Then there was Otis. At seventy-three, Otis was easily the oldest person in the diner, and he loved telling stories. Most of the stories Otis told were made up. Some of the true ones had a bit of fabrication thrown in for entertainment's sake.

Kyle focused on this conversation as he opened the folder and plucked a pencil from his shirt pocket.

"God's honest truth!" Otis said. "She came running out the house with a shotgun, smoke from her cigarette fillin' up her one good eye, her other eye swoll shut and bleeding from where that brick hit her, and she tryna load that thing as she run across the yard."

Ray, Bobby, and Eric, the other three occupants of Otis's booth, were captivated by the story as if it were their first time hearing it.

"Then what?" an excited Eric asked.

"Don't rush me!" Otis exclaimed. "I'm gettin' to it! So, she tryna put them shells in, but she can't see. By now, them boys are runnin' back to the car and jumpin' through the windows. She looks up and yells, 'Come on back! I got somethin' for you!' Then she slams the barrel up, and BANG! She pulls the trigger. The back window shatters all over the street!"

Everyone in the booth roared with laughter. Otis sat back, smiling, pleased with himself.

"You telling that story again, old man?"

Kyle turned to the voice and noticed Mike seated at the bar, holding a cup of coffee and a newspaper.

"Mind your business, Mike! Ain't no one talkin' to you!" Otis said.

Across from Kyle, a small face popped up over the bench. "Is it done?"

3

Kyle smiled. "Good morning, Molly."

"Sorry," Molly said. "I keep forgetting my manners. Good morning." She folded her arms over the backrest and rested her chin on them. "So, is it?"

After a quick glance at the paper, he turned the drawing so she could view it.

Her eyes grew wide. "It's beautiful. Mom's gonna love it."

"I hope so."

"When are you gonna give it to her?"

That's a good question.

"I'm not sure. When the time is right."

"You should do it today."

"Oh? And why's that?"

"She's having a bad day. Dad pissed her off again."

Kyle frowned. "You know, that's not appropriate language for a young lady like you."

She lifted her head. "I'm nine. I'm practically an adult."

He smiled. "'Practically?' That's a big word."

She smiled back. "My teacher says I'm the smartest kid in class."

"I believe it. Speaking of teachers, why aren't you in school?"

"It's a teacher workday." Her head tilted to the side, and her eyes narrowed. "Which doesn't even make sense. Teachers work every day. Why don't they call it 'teacher break day' or something like that? I mean, they're taking a break, right?"

"I can't argue with that logic."

"Anyway, my dad was supposed to pick me up, but mom said he's probably drunk at some floozie's house." Something grabbed her attention, and she glanced to her left. "Hi, mom. I was having a phili… a philis… a conversation with the sheriff."

Lauren stopped next to Kyle's table, notepad in hand. "Philosophical?"

"Yeah. That."

Lauren smiled. "What about?"

"We were discussing why teachers get to take breaks, but they have to work anyway."

"I see. And what was the resolution?"

"There wasn't one. You interrupted before we could finish."

Lauren pulled a pencil from the pocket of her pink and white smock. "Well, that was rude of me, wasn't it?"

"It totally was."

She turned to Kyle. "Good morning, Kyle. I hope she isn't bothering you too much?"

"Not at all. I rather enjoy these little conversations."

Molly grinned. "Of course you do. I'm adorable."

Lauren chuckled. "What can I get you?"

Kyle glanced down and realized that the drawing was out in full view. He quickly covered it with the folder.

"Can I just get some coffee and bacon, please?"

She nodded and repeated his order. "The breakfast of champions. Coming right up."

He watched as she turned and headed toward the counter. She was graceful, almost magical, as she retrieved a mug from under the counter and a pot of coffee from a hotplate, then brought them back to his booth. He noticed something different about her as she set down the cup and poured the drink.

"You cut your hair," he said.

"I did. You like it?"

He took a sip of coffee. "I do. It looks nice."

Molly was watching the encounter closely, grinning.

"Thanks." Lauren looked down at the folder. The corner of the drawing was peeking out from the edge. "So, when are you going to show me your latest masterpiece?"

"When it's done."

"I hope so." She smiled again. "I've always liked your artwork."

He placed his hand on the folder and readied himself for what came next.

Molly perked up.

A voice called out from the radio that was clipped to his belt. "Kyle, you there?"

It was Leo, one of his deputies.

He unclipped the radio, brought it close to his mouth, and pressed the button on the side. "Leo, what's up?"

"I got a call from Beverly. She wants you to call her. She said it's important."

Beverly was one of his mom's closest friends and the owner of Beverly's Inn, a quaint bed-and-breakfast just outside of town.

"Did she say what she needed?"

"No. Just that it was important."

"Copy. Thanks, Leo."

He set the radio on the table and pushed himself from the bench seat. "You mind if I use your phone?"

"Not at all," Lauren answered.

He crossed the short distance to the telephone hanging on the wall next to the kitchen, then brought the receiver to his ear as he dialed the number from memory.

It rang three times before a woman answered. "Hello?"

"Beverly. It's Kyle. Is everything okay?"

"No, not really. I need your help."

He listened intently, nodding as if she could see him. "Okay. I'll be right there." He replaced the phone into its cradle returned to the booth.

Lauren smiled. "Duty calls?"

"Yeah. Can I get that to go?"

She picked up the coffee mug and turned back toward the counter. Kyle slid the drawing from under the folder and studied it. He had captured her face so perfectly that it could have been a photograph. Every strand of hair, every freckle on her face, her cute little nose, all captured in #2 graphite.

Molly frowned at him. "Give it to her."

"Next time."

"Chicken."

He slid the drawing back into the folder, tucked it underneath his arm, and grabbed the briefcase. Lauren met him at the door, a paper coffee cup with a plastic lid in one hand and a brown paper bag in the other.

"I threw some bagels in there, too," she said.

"Thank you."

Noticing that his hands were full, she opened the door for him.

He turned to say goodbye to Molly and saw her standing on the bench seat, thumbs hooked into her armpits. She started flapping her arms like a bird. He stuck his tongue out at her, and she replied in kind. He smiled at Lauren as he walked past. "Thank you again."

"Any time, Deputy."

He crossed the street, placed the bag and cup on the hood of his car, then opened the driver's door. He turned and saw Lauren still standing in the doorway. She waved. He waved back. Someone walked up behind him, and he turned to see Otis.

"When you gonna ask that young lady out, Deputy? You know she ain't gonna wait forever."

"Mind your business, Otis."

4

Kyle stood on the porch of Beverly's Inn, gazing out across a golden-brown wheat field. A few miles beyond that, the trees on Chester Mountain displayed vibrant reds, oranges, and yellows.

Somewhere to his right, a hawk screeched. He closed his eyes and listened to the otherwise peaceful surroundings. He always loved coming here, escaping the noise of the town, however small it was.

The door opened behind him, and a well-dressed, middle-aged woman stood in the doorway, a look of concern on her face. "Kyle. Thank you for coming." He turned to face Beverly. Her shoulder-length, wavy brown hair was showing strands of white. She wiped her hands down the front of her blue apron before pulling him in for a brief hug. When she let go, she took a step back. "Sorry, I'm a mess. I was cleaning up."

"Of course," he said, "Where is it?" She led him inside. He removed his sheriff's hat, hung it on the post inside the door, and followed her to the second floor.

"You said on the phone that she checked in two days ago?" he asked.

"That's right. Tuesday afternoon." She reached the top step, stopped on the landing, and motioned to a door that had a small metal plate affixed to it that said simply "B" in a capital, script-style font. He followed her gaze to the door, nodded, and reached for the handle. Beverly turned away as it swung open.

The sun shone through the window on the far side of the room, casting a warm glow. Shadows playfully danced against the walls as a breeze flowed through the curtains. Kyle immediately locked onto a bloodstain on the bed.

A small pool of blood on the floor, halfway between the bed and the window, also caught his attention, and he noticed that the window had been broken from the inside.

He turned back toward Beverly. "This is how you found it?"

She was still on the landing, her back to him. She looked over her shoulder when she answered. "Yes. She asked for a seven o'clock wake-up for this morning, but she didn't answer the phone, so I came up and knocked on the door. It wasn't closed all the way. I saw that... mess... and called you."

"Why don't you go downstairs? You don't need to see this."

"I'll make coffee." She headed back down the stairs.

When he entered the room, he noticed a small travel bag on the floor next to the window, just large enough for about three days of clothing. Beside the bed was a nightstand, where a hairbrush was placed next to a lamp. He pulled a pair of blue latex gloves from his back pocket and slipped them on, then pulled open the nightstand drawer. It was empty. He crossed the room, picked up the travel bag, set it on the corner of the bed opposite the blood, and unzipped it.

He carefully removed each item and set them on the bed: two pairs of jeans, one pair of shorts, three pairs of ladies' underwear, three bras, and three pairs of socks, all neatly folded. On one side, he discovered a green wallet in a zippered pouch and pulled it out.

He repacked the clothing as he had found it, then placed the bag on the floor under the window.

The wallet contained two credit cards, $50 cash, and a Colorado driver's license. "Melissa Harmon," he read. "What happened here, Melissa?" He tucked the license back into the wallet and slid it into his pocket.

He raised the Polaroid camera that was hanging around his neck and took pictures of everything in the room from every angle, tucking each picture into his shirt pocket. Satisfied that he'd gotten everything, he stepped out into the hall. After one last look, he closed the door, took another step back, and took a picture of the door.

On his right was another room for rent. That door was wide open. To his left was the shared bathroom. There was nothing notable in there that he could see. Everything was clean; the sink was dry, and the towels were unused. The medicine chest behind the mirror was empty. He took pictures of it all, just in case, then went downstairs.

5

Beverly was sitting at the kitchen island, sipping a freshly brewed coffee. She set down the cup and slid another one toward him. He pulled the green wallet from his pocket, retrieved the license, and held it up.

"Is this your tenant?"

"Um, no, it's not." Her brow furrowed as she studied the ID. "I mean, it's the same name, but that ain't her."

He returned the ID and wallet to his pocket and retrieved a small notepad and a pen from his shirt. "Can you describe her?"

"She was mid-twenties to early thirties, average height for a woman. Maybe 5'6, 5'7. Brown hair to here." She brushed her fingertips against the top of her shoulder. "Brown eyes."

"According to the ID, Melissa has blue eyes and blonde hair. She's 5'3 tall and is..." He did the math: "19 years old."

"There's something else." Beverly rose from the stool and left the room.

When she returned a moment later, she carried an oversized book, which she set on the island and flipped open. "The guest register. Look here." She pointed to the last entry.

He glanced at the printed name and signature.

Melissa Harmon.

"The signature doesn't match the license." He took a picture of the page. "Thank you. I'm gonna go take a look at that window from outside. Why don't you stay here? I'll let you know when I'm done."

She nodded and took the book back to her desk.

He retrieved his hat from the hook and then made his way to the back of the house, where he found a small debris field of broken glass under the second-story window. He kneeled beside what looked like dried blood and captured several close-up photos, then looked up at the window. Scuff marks marred the off-white siding just underneath, as if someone had hung there and tried to gain a foothold.

He rose, took a few steps back, and imagined someone falling from the window and landing in the exact spot as the small pool of blood on the ground. The shattered glass strewn all around looked consistent with something, or someone, being pushed or thrown through the window.

Taking in the entire scene, he noticed a few drops of blood about a foot away. Then another foot beyond that. In fact, he saw they made a trail across the yard and into the woods. He followed as far as he could, then lost the trail inside the tree line.

He unclipped the radio from his belt. "Control, this is Deputy Lorne."

Less than three seconds passed before he got a response. "Hey Kyle, it's Betty."

"Betty, can you call Carl and have him meet me at Beverly's?"

"I'll call him, but it's his day off. He's not gonna like it."

"Tell him to bring Marley."

There was a brief silence, then, "Marley?"

"I need her nose."

Betty was quiet again for a moment. "Copy that, Sheriff. I'll call him right now."

He was about to remind her for the millionth time he wasn't the sheriff but gave up halfway through the thought. It wouldn't do any good. It never did.

He headed back toward his patrol car. When he rounded the corner of the inn, he almost walked right into Beverly. She held up the coffee cup she'd offered him before.

"Thank you," he said. "Whatever happened inside, it spilled out into the backyard. Did you hear anything last night?"

"No, I wasn't here. I was having dinner with Bea and Dorthea at Hannigan's. I didn't get home until late. Maybe eleven thirty? I went straight to bed."

"What time did you leave here?"

"I'd say five thirty, five forty-five." She tried to look around him, at the backyard.

"It's a mess. Glass everywhere. And more blood."

"That poor girl." She was visibly upset. "What happened to her?"

"I wish I knew."

A voice called over the radio. "Sheriff, it's Betty."

Kyle frowned as he pressed his thumb into the transmit button. "Betty, I'm not the sheriff."

"I know."

Beverly chuckled at that.

"Carl said he'll be right there."

"Copy. Thank you."

"You're welcome, Sheriff."

He let out a long sigh and saw that Beverly was trying, and failing, to suppress a grin.

"Have you given them an answer yet? About the job?"

"No." He clipped the radio to his belt.

"You need to, before they hire someone else."

He shrugged. "I know. But I'm not even sure that I want it."

"You're already doing the job. You might as well let them pay you for it."

"This is true. But I think it might be time for a career change."

"Career change? I've known you since you were in diapers. You've never wanted to do anything else. What are you talking about, career change? What would you even do?"

That is an excellent question.

"I don't know. Something."

"What happened wasn't your fault. You know that."

"I know. Still..." He diverted his gaze back toward Chester Mountain. Beverly turned and followed where he was looking. Fog was rolling in over the trees.

6

A dark green pickup pulled into the driveway and parked behind Kyle's patrol car. Carl climbed from the driver's seat and went to the rear of the truck, where Marley eagerly awaited his attention. He opened the cage, and the three-year-old beagle jumped down. When she saw Beverly, she ran over and sat at her feet, her tail wagging a hundred miles a minute.

Beverly kneeled, grabbed Marley's head with both hands and scratched behind her ears. "Hello, pretty girl."

Carl came up to them. "Kyle, Beverly."

"Carl. You got here quick," Kyle said.

Carl adjusted his brown camouflaged hat, which matched his cargo pants. His blaze orange hunter's vest was zipped up to the neck. "Me and the boys were just up the road fixin' to flush out some birds on Emmett's land."

"Thank you for taking the time. It's back here." He led Carl to the back of the house and showed him what he'd found, then they walked to the tree line. "This is where I lost the trail."

Carl nodded, then called out, "Marley! Here, girl!"

She came bounding around the corner and ran full speed toward them, her big ears flopping. She stopped at Carl's feet and sat, looking up at him. Carl put his hand on the ground next to a droplet of blood. Marley's nose dropped, and she picked up a scent. She looked back up at Carl.

"Go!" She bolted into the woods, Carl and Kyle following right behind.

Marley zig-zagged through the trees, sniffing the ground frantically as she tried to follow the trail. She jumped over a stump and ducked under a fallen tree. Each time she came upon another drop of blood, she announced her location with two sharp barks before running off toward the next one.

"Damn, she's fast!" Kyle struggled to keep up, but he could no longer see her, and her howling sounded like she was miles away. "I don't see her."

"Right there." Carl pointed off to the right. Kyle followed his outstretched arm and saw her jump over a log before she disappeared again. They changed their course and ran in that direction.

They heard her baying somewhere in the distance, and they exchanged glances. "She found something," Carl said.

The woods ended, and they found themselves on a dirt road. Marley was sitting a few feet from a body, which lay just out of reach of a car. She wagged her tail ferociously and pointed her head straight up as she sang into the sky.

"Marley, come!" Carl called out. She turned and bounded toward him. "Good girl." He rubbed her back and offered her a treat from his other hand.

Kyle examined the body as he approached. It was male, average build, with brown hair. He was lying face down on the road. Three bloody holes were visible on the back of his gray jacket.

The car was empty. Keys were hanging from the lock of the open trunk, and the rear driver's side door was open.

Kyle reached down and rolled the man over. Three bullet holes dotted his chest, a mirror image of the ones on his back. The man's chest rose as a labored breath escaped him.

"Hang on, Mister. We got you."

7

Erica watched from the trees as the cop rolled the body over. At this distance, she couldn't tell if he was still alive. She ducked and covered her head with the hood of her pullover as the scene played out below her.

The two men lifted the body from the ground and placed him into the back seat of the car, then the cop grabbed the keys from the trunk and slammed it shut. He dropped into the driver's seat, and the engine came to life.

She watched, helpless, as her means of escape spun around on the dirt road and sped off, leaving behind the second man and the dog.

It was suddenly eerily quiet.

The man reached down and clipped a leash to the dog's collar.

The beagle's ears perked up, and its head snapped around, looking right at her. The animal let out a low, throaty growl, and the man looked up the hill, scanning the trees. His hand slowly fell to a pistol holstered on his belt.

"Come on, girl, let's get out of here." He gently tugged the leash, and they disappeared into the woods.

She tucked the small revolver into the pocket of her pullover and concluded that he must still be alive. Why else would that cop rush off like that?

She needed to find him.

She waited a while before crossing the dirt road and making her way back to the inn, then stopped just inside the tree line and watched the house for a few minutes. Shadows were moving around in the upstairs room. The silhouette of a woman – *Beverly?* – placed something in the window that blocked her view. Deciding it was safe enough to get closer, she jogged up to the old house and peered around the corner.

A police car sat in the driveway. She sprinted over to it and peered through the window; the keys were in the ignition.

And why wouldn't they be? A small-time police department like this? Who would ever think of stealing their one cruiser?

She opened the door and slid into the driver's seat.

Fifteen minutes later, she slowed the car as she approached the city limits sign that read "Millhaven, Tennessee. Population 953." She pulled the car to a stop on the side of the road and shut off the engine.

As she placed the keys on the front seat, she opened the door, pressed the lock button, and stepped out.

8

Kyle paced in front of the nurse's station, looking down at his pocket notebook, trying to recall every detail about the scene where he'd found the car: the position of the body, the direction the car had been facing, the open trunk, and rear driver's side door. Usually, he would have taken photos of everything, but given the circumstances…

His radio hissed. "Sheriff, it's Betty."

"Betty…" He didn't even attempt to hide his displeasure at the title.

"Sorry, Kyle."

"What have you got?" He set his notepad on the counter, clicked his pen closed, and slid it into the slot in his shirt pocket.

"Andy is on his way to the hospital to get the car, and he'll take you back to Beverly's. He wants you to meet him outside."

"Thanks. How long?"

"He said about five minutes. He's just around the corner."

"Thank you. Can you call Carl and have him come to the station? I need him to give a statement."

"Sure thing."

His pager vibrated in his pocket, and he dug it out. He recognized Mayor Hawthorne's number.

"Thanks, Betty. I'll check in later." He crossed to the nurse's station. "Mind if I use your phone?"

She shook her head as she continued typing on her keyboard, not bothering to look up.

The mayor answered right away.

"Good morning, sir. It's Kyle."

"Kyle, I'm glad you called. As you know, the elections are coming up, and we need an answer. If you're not going to accept, we'll need to move forward with other options."

"Mayor, with respect, this is not a good time."

"It never is with you, is it, *Deputy*?" He drew out the last word as if reminding Kyle for whom he worked.

He sighed. "I found a body near Beverly's this morning. And we have a missing person. A young woman. I don't know how they tie in together yet, but I'm working on it."

The line was silent.

Did he hang up?

"Excellent! Kyle, you solve this case, and you're a shoo-in for sheriff! Keep me informed!" The line went dead. Kyle pulled the phone from his ear and stared at it.

"Unbelievable." He hadn't decided if he even wanted the job, but for some reason, everyone just assumed he would take it.

He felt a migraine coming on. He looked at the nurse sitting behind the desk. "Call me if anything changes?"

"Of course, I'll let the doctor know."

He handed her the phone, thanked her, then headed to the exit and stepped outside in time to see a red rollback pull into the parking lot. He waved to Andy, who nodded in acknowledgment. The truck stopped beside the light-blue four-door sedan parked outside the emergency room entrance.

Andy had the car secured to the flatbed of his truck in no time. After a relatively short, silent ride, they arrived at the first crime scene, and Kyle felt perplexed by what he saw as they pulled into the driveway - or rather, what he *didn't* see.

This can't be happening again.

This was the third time, and there was no way he'd be able to live this one down.

"Where the hell's my car?"

9

Erica admired the flower arrangements in the window. The iris was always her favorite. She remembered when she was younger, her mom would take her to their 'secret place,' a field that was filled with them. They would sit on a blanket, have lunch, and enjoy the peace and quiet.

As she closed her eyes, she was transported back to that simpler time when her biggest worry was what color dress to wear to school.

A car drove past, bringing her back to the present.

Inside the store, an elderly woman carefully arranged flowers in a vase, ensuring that each one was placed just right before setting the arrangement on the counter.

Her stomach growled, and she realized that she hadn't eaten anything all day. She caught the diner's reflection behind her in the window.

My wallet is back at the inn. I don't have any money.

Crossing the street, she spotted an old, red pickup turn the corner. It parked in front of the diner, and she recognized Otis when he got out. He stretched his arms above his head and twisted his body left and right before pushing through the glass doors.

Moving toward a phone booth, she looked both ways, surveying the street. She pulled the hoodie over her head and turned her attention back to the red pickup. The WWII Army Veteran's license plate read MOONSHN.

Very subtle, Otis.

A car approached, and she ducked inside the booth, picked up the receiver, and held it to her ear.

Behind her, the diner door opened with a *ding*, and she cautiously peered over her shoulder. Otis was carrying a brown paper bag in one hand and a white Styrofoam cup in the other as he stepped off the sidewalk. She saw that he had a limp and was slightly hunched over. Time was not treating him all that well.

He opened the truck's passenger door and placed the bag and cup on the seat. She hung up the phone, stepped out of the booth, and took a few steps toward him.

"Mister Otis."

Otis turned. It took a moment before recognition set in. "Erica? That really you?"

Erica nodded. He grabbed her shoulders and pulled her close into a firm hug.

"Let me look at you, child!" He pushed her back to arm's length. His smile faded as he examined her face. "What is it?"

"I'm in trouble. I need help."

"What's going on?"

She glanced back over her shoulder. A man and woman strolled toward them on the sidewalk. She pulled the hood lower over her face.

Otis ushered her toward the truck. "Get in. Let's get someplace more quiet."

10

Kyle hung his hat on the peg attached to the wall as he entered the sheriff's station. He raised his paper cup and sipped the lukewarm drink as he headed toward his office.

"Morning, Sheriff," Betty called from her desk. He glanced up at her as she tilted her head toward the corner, to his glass-walled office. Her curly blonde hair was tied into a loose ponytail. "You have a visitor."

Visitor?

"Who is it?" he asked.

"Detective from Chicago."

"Chicago?"

He scanned the office, looking for the other deputy on duty. They were a small department in a small town. The department had five deputies, himself included: two were on duty during the day, and the others rotated the evening and overnight hours.

"Rios," he said.

Serena Rios looked up from her laptop, a steaming paper cup identical to his mere inches from her mouth. She raised her eyebrows. "Yes, Boss?"

"Can you put out an APB on my cruiser?"

"Dios mio. Did you lose it again?"

He shot her a look.

She sighed. "I'll call Annie Willis, too. Maybe Arnie and Wes took it for a joyride again."

He nodded as he crossed the room to his office, where he found a well-dressed man sitting behind his desk in the sheriff's chair. The stranger's brown skin was a stark contrast to his pink button-down shirt with a white collar and cuffs. He closed the door behind him.

"Deputy Lorne," he introduced himself, "Acting sheriff. You are?"

The man winced slightly as he rose from the chair. "Jack." He held out his hand, and Kyle noticed what appeared to be a bandage peeking out from his sleeve. "Detective Jack Pearce."

Kyle shook his hand. "From Chicago? What brings you to our little town?"

"I'm looking for someone. A fugitive. I have reason to believe she's here."

"What makes you think that?"

"You ran a search for a missing person."

"Melissa Harmon?"

Jack reached for a manilla folder on the desk and held it out. Kyle took it and flipped open the cover. On the right side, a paper clip held a police report in place; on the left, a blown-up copy of a driver's license.

"What happened to your face?" Kyle asked as he began reading the report.

Jack touched the days-old cut on his cheek. "I tracked my fugitive to a bus station outside Chicago. She's a suspected drug trafficker who, we believe, killed her supplier. She attacked me and got away." He paused. "Then, she assaulted Miss Harmon and took her bag. Now, since I know for a fact that Miss Harmon is in a hospital back home, as soon as I saw her name pop up, I figured it was a safe bet that my fugitive was here." He pulled a piece of paper from his back pocket and unfolded it. He inspected it briefly before handing it to Kyle. "This is her. We got this off a camera at the bus station."

Kyle took the photo. He noticed the size difference between her and the detective.

There's no way she could have overpowered a man his size.

"She definitely matches the description of my missing person. She have a name?"

"Probably, but I don't know it. I've been calling her Jane."

"Jane." Kyle returned Melissa's license photo to the folder before handing the folder back. He held up the photo of Jane. "Mind if I make a copy?"

"Keep it. I have more."

Kyle nodded, turned, and reached for the door. He pulled it open and took a quick look back. "I have an errand to run, but I'm driving out to the inn this afternoon. I want to take another look at the scene and see if my witness remembers anything else. You want to come along?"

"Love to."

"I'll meet you outside, in our parking lot. Two o'clock?"

"I'll be there."

Jack left the office and crossed through the bullpen toward the front door. As he went, Kyle noticed he was favoring his left leg.

"Were you in an accident?" Kyle asked.

Jack stopped and turned to face him. "Sorry?"

"Your limp. The bandage on your arm. Were you in an accident?"

"Oh, that." His eyes shifted from Kyle to Serena to Betty, then back to Kyle. He shook his head. "Slipped in the shower. Hurt like a mother." He smiled, then turned and continued toward the door.

Kyle nodded. Serena was across the room, tacking a photo of a missing girl to the BOLO board. "Another one?" he asked.

She nodded. "Afraid so. This one from Lee County up in Virginia."

He read the information on the notice. "Fifteen years old. Damn."

"Been missing for three days. They're expanding the search to ten miles, but they asked us to keep an eye out, too, just in case."

He held out Janes' security camera photo. "Here's one more. This one's more local."

She took it from him. "Jesu Cristo. Are you serious?"

"Last seen at Beverly's two nights ago. Can you make copies and circulate it to everyone?"

She took the photo from him. "Of course."

"And contact Chicago PD; see if you can get some info on Detective Jack Pearce." She looked up at him. "There's something about him," he continued, "Doesn't feel right."

11

"Have you given any thought to what I said last week?" Carolyn tapped the tip of her pencil against the notepad on her lap. She reached up with her other hand, brushed a strand of red hair from her face, and tucked it behind her ear.

Kyle recalled their last conversation as he focused his attention on the orange string on the arm of the chair. It was wrapped around his left index finger so tightly that the tip of the finger was turning red. He tugged it, but it didn't budge. "I have, and it does make sense."

"Are you saying that because you think it's what I want to hear?"

He let the string slip from his finger and tried a different tactic: He grasped it between his thumb and forefinger and pulled as hard as he could, only succeeding in giving himself a rub burn on his thumb. Placing the wound against his lips, he felt that it was warm and it was throbbing. "No, I thought about it, and I do agree."

"Because of what happened, or because it's what you want?"

That's a good question.

"Your hesitation is your answer." Carolyn set the notepad on the arm of her chair, crossed one leg over the other, and smoothed out the fabric of her blue skirt. "Last week, we had a breakthrough. I'd like to talk about that."

He nodded. "Okay."

"The night your father died, you two were in his office, discussing his retirement."

He nodded again.

"Things got heated."

"He told me I wasn't good enough to take his place."

"You said he told you…" She looked down at her notes. "'You're not

27

ready,' and 'you need more experience.'"

"Yes."

She grasped the edge of her glasses between her middle finger and thumb and adjusted them on her nose. "And that's when it happened."

As he closed his eyes, he was instantly transported back to that night. He could smell the aroma of stale coffee and feel the smooth coolness of the leather chair. He took a long, slow breath. "He was gone before the ambulance arrived."

"And you blame yourself for that?"

"We were both yelling. I should have just walked away."

"It's not your fault he had a heart attack. It would have happened regardless."

"Maybe." He wrapped the string around his finger again and gave it a few gentle tugs.

She jotted some notes on the pad, then set the pencil back down. "Two issues I see here. First, you blame yourself for his death. Second, you believe that he thought you weren't, as you put it, 'good enough' to be the sheriff after he retired."

"That's what he said."

"So, which was it? You're not good enough, or you're not experienced enough?"

"I know what he said, but I also know what he meant."

"Maybe what he said was exactly what he meant." Carolyn jotted a few more notes. "You said that my suggestion made sense. Does that help make your decision any easier?"

He gave up on the string and met her gaze. "Yes."

"And?"

"Regardless of what my dad said or didn't say, the meaning was clear: I'm not ready."

"Do you agree with that statement?"

He nodded. "Yes. Yes, I do."

"You've been a deputy for what? Five years?"

"Five years last month."

"And it's been four months since you were promoted to acting sheriff."

He nodded.

"In that time, how do you think you've been doing?"

"Okay." He shifted in the chair. Temporarily admitting defeat, he smoothed the errant string against the fabric of the chair, trying to blend it between the ridges of the material.

"Apparently, so do a lot of others. Your coworkers follow your directions without hesitation; the mayor offered you the position full-time."

"Yes."

"So maybe you are ready."

"Maybe that's true. But if I don't think I'm ready, am I really ready?"

She smiled. "You're starting to sound like a therapist."

"Mayor Hawthorne wants me to do a campaign commercial."

"Oh?"

He nodded.

"Are you excited about that, at least?"

"Not really. He wants to use that old place up on Chester Mountain."

Her eyes grew wide. "The abandoned TV set? Is that still up there?"

"It's still there. We drive through there now and then, make sure the kids haven't gotten themselves hurt."

She smiled. "I haven't thought about that place in years."

"He wants me to dress up in an old-west cowboy outfit and talk about my dad, how my family is old-fashioned, and all that."

"No offense to our dear mayor, but that sounds like a horrible idea."

"I agree. Anyway, to get back to your question. I'm working on a case right now. When it's over, I think I'll use up some of my vacation. Refocus, recharge, and see where my head is afterward."

"And the job?"

"I'll probably pass. If it comes up again later, I'll re-evaluate my situation. Then... who knows?"

She glanced up at the clock. "My next appointment should be here in a few minutes," she said.

He rose from the chair. "Thank you for squeezing me in."

She stood. "Of course. My door is always open."

She followed him to the door. He reached out and grabbed the knob, pulled the door open, and paused. He looked back at the orange chair, then walked over to it as he pulled a Swiss Army knife from his pocket. After flipping the knife blade from the tool, he grasped the loose string, pulled it tight, and swiped the blade across it.

He held the now-liberated string up so she could see it. "Can I have this?"

She smiled at him. "Sure. I think you've earned it."

12

Erica bounced in the seat as the pickup rumbled along the dirt road. She smiled, recalling the times she and Otis's grandson, Floyd, made this trip when they were younger. They would exaggerate each bounce, counting the times they hit their head on the ceiling of the truck. They were best friends, inseparable from each other. "Whatever happened to Floyd?"

Otis glanced at her. He pressed the eject button on the 8-track, halting Billie Holiday's *I'll Be Seeing You.* "You been gone a long time. Floyd went off and joined the army. He's flyin' helicopters in Bosnia."

"Bosnia? And a pilot? I never would've imagined."

"He always said he was gonna be a motorcycle racer."

She laughed. "He couldn't even ride a bike!"

Otis chuckled. "He's a special one, that boy. Wasn't very coordinated, but he sure had dreams."

She smiled as she turned back to the window, just in time to see a fawn run into the safety of the trees.

"He asks about you all the time."

"He does?"

"Of course! Misses you somthin' fierce. He got some leave comin' up. Said he gon' be home in the spring. Maybe you stick around and see him?"

She closed her eyes. The sweet melody from years gone by was still going through her mind. "I'd like that."

As they came to the end of the road, Otis slowed the truck and they stopped in front of an old two-story cabin. Its porch spanned the entire front, and a garden filled with tall sunflowers rested on either side of the steps.

"It's just how I remembered it. Only, it looks smaller."

Otis shifted the gear lever into park and shut off the engine. He turned to face her. "You hungry?"

"Starving."

As they exited the truck and started toward the cabin, she could see that time had not been kind to it. The wood was rotting in places, and one window on the side was covered with boards.

"Last windstorm knocked a branch through that. Nearly went through the house. Only place has a replacement is in Bristol."

"You can't get one local?"

"I can, but that's old glass. Hand-poured. Want to keep it original."

She nodded. As he climbed the steps and opened the front door, Erica caught a whiff of a peculiar smell on the breeze. "Mr. Otis," she paused. "Are you... is that..."

He grinned. "Moonshine."

"Of course it is."

13

Kyle turned his Jeep Wrangler into the driveway of Beverly's Inn, passing a large evergreen on the right. In his rearview, he saw Jack's dark blue sedan follow him in. He pulled into the parking space closest to the porch and shut off the car. As he exited the Jeep, the sedan stopped in the next spot over.

"That was one hell of a view," Jack said as he climbed out of the car and closed the door, "Coming over that mountain like that. I could see the whole town!"

"One of our many hidden secrets."

"I've never seen so many deer. And were those wild turkeys in that field?"

Kyle grinned. "Yes, they were."

As they climbed the steps to the Inn, the door opened, and Beverly greeted them. "Kyle. I wasn't expecting to see you again today. And who might this be?"

Before Kyle could reply, Jack closed the gap and held out his hand. "Detective Jack Pearce, Chicago PD."

Beverly gave a quizzical look as she took his hand. "Chicago?"

"We're here about the missing girl," Kyle said. "Mind if we take another look at the room?"

"Not at all. There's not much left to look at after your deputies cleaned it out but help yourself. Would you gentlemen like some tea?"

"I'd love some," Jack said. He followed Beverly through the door, Kyle right behind him. Jack stopped just inside.

Kyle nodded toward the stairs just to their right. "Up there."

They found the door wide open, and the window was covered with a square of particle board. Kyle flipped the switch inside the door, and the ceiling light came on.

A large swatch of the carpet was missing, as well as the padding underneath, and the mattress from the bed was gone.

Kyle pulled a stack of photos from a folder and handed them to Jack. "This is what it looked like when I first arrived."

Jack took the photos and flipped through them, holding each one up and matching it to the room. He crossed to the far corner to see everything from a different angle. "There was a bag here." He pointed to the spot where Kyle had found the travel bag.

"Yes." He scanned the room, imagining what could have played out that night.

"Anything interesting in it?"

Kyle shook his head. "Just clothes, a little bit of cash, two credit cards, and a driver's license."

"Melissa Harmon?"

Kyle nodded.

Jack pried the particle board away from the window as far as he could. "Long way down." He handed the photos back.

Kyle took them. "Yes, it is."

14

When they returned to the first floor, they found Beverly in the dining room, setting the table with four place settings. "I have a family coming in from Wichita tonight. They should be here in a couple of hours."

Jack leaned against the doorjamb. "This is a beautiful place you got here."

"Thank you. It's been in my family for four generations. It was my mother who turned it into an Inn." She picked up a glass of amber liquid and held it out for him. "Your tea."

"Much appreciated."

She handed Kyle a similar glass.

"You said that the night of the incident, you were gone from about five thirty until eleven thirty?" Kyle asked.

"Around that, yes."

"And you were with Dorthea and Bea?"

"Yes." She looked down at her hand and began scraping at one of her fingernails. "At the diner."

Kyle recalled the original conversation. "I thought you said you went to Hannigan's?"

Beverly turned her head and tilted it to the side. "Maybe it was. I forget things sometimes."

"This was two nights ago," Jack said. "You don't remember where you went for dinner two nights ago?"

"Hell," Beverly said. "I don't remember what I had for breakfast some days."

Jack and Kyle exchanged a glance, then Kyle pulled the photo from his pocket and handed it to her. "Does this woman look familiar?"

"Yes. That's Melissa Harmon. Well, the woman who checked in as Melissa Harmon."

"You're sure?" Jack asked.

She nodded and handed the paper back to Kyle. He refolded the photo and tapped a corner against his palm.

"Do you know her real name?" She asked.

"Not yet. We're calling her Jane." Jack answered.

"Jane. I hope she's okay. That poor girl. I hope you find her."

"We're doing everything we can," Kyle said. He slid the folded paper back into his pocket. "We're gonna have a look outside." He handed her his half-empty glass. "Thank you for the drink."

She took the glass and set it on the counter behind her, then turned back and took Jack's glass, which was empty.

"Thank you. That tea was delicious."

"Thank *you*. If I can be of any more help…"

Kyle led the way to the door. Once they were outside, rounding the corner, Jack said, "She's holding something back."

Kyle looked over at him. "I hate to say this, but I agree. Her story changed."

"You know where we can find these two young ladies she says she was with? Bea and Dorthea?"

"I have a very good idea."

When they reached the back of the house, Kyle noticed little yellow flags sticking out of the ground, each numbered from nine to fifteen, marking a trail from the impact spot under the window to the tree line.

"That's quite the fall," Jack said. He stood just outside the circle of flags, looking up at the boarded-up window. "How could anyone survive that?"

"Must've had a guardian angel," Kyle said. He turned and pointed at the flags leading to the woods. "We followed the trail that way. Found him lying on the ground just a few feet from a car."

"Damn."

"He was in bad shape, but he was still alive. By the time I got him to the hospital… I have no idea if he's going to make it."

"I'd really like to meet this man."

"So would I," Kyle said. "Maybe he can tell us what happened out here."

15

Erica took a bite of the country ham biscuit, savoring the saltiness of the ham and the sweetness of the bread. "I haven't tasted anything like this in years."

Otis placed a glass of iced tea next to her plate and sat in the chair across the table from her. He waited as she finished one biscuit, then started another. "From the looks of it, you ain't eat much of anything in a while."

She took a sip of tea. "Thank you. That was delicious."

Otis nodded. "Now, why don't you tell me what's got you so scared, you come runnin' back home after all these years?"

She hesitated for a moment. "I saw something I wasn't supposed to see."

"Somethin' bad?"

"Something very bad." She took a breath and held it for a few seconds.

How much do I tell him? Can I trust him to know the whole truth?

She decided it was best to leave some things out. "I was on my way home from work, and I cut through an alley to get to the bus stop." She took another sip of tea. "I saw two men down a side alley. They were arguing. One of them pulled a knife and stabbed the other one."

Otis's eyes grew wider. "Lord."

"My whole body started shaking. I dropped my drink, and the man turned and saw me. He started coming toward me, and I ran."

"Did you go to the police?"

She looked up at him. "He *was* the police. He had a gold badge around his neck."

"So, what you do?"

"I ran home. The next day, I saw a news report on the TV. They had a drawing of my face. They said *I* killed that man in the alley."

"So, you kept runnin'."

She nodded. "I didn't know what to do. I packed a bag and went straight to the bus station. I called Keith and…"

"Keith?"

"My fiancé. He told me to get the first bus out of Chicago, and he'd meet me as soon as he could." Her eyes met his. "There was a young woman. Early twenties, I think. At the bus station. She tried to help me get away from him."

"What happened?"

She took a breath. "I think he killed her."

Otis leaned across the table and placed his hand on hers.

"He somehow found us at the inn here in Millhaven. Keith tried to stop him. He…" She buried her face in her hands, and the tears finally came. "I don't know what happened to him," she said between sobs. "A policeman showed up and took him away. I was watching from the trees. I was too scared to move. I don't even know if he's still alive."

Otis leaned back in the chair and stroked his chin. "You can stay as long as you need. We'll see if we can find that fiancé of yours."

16

The diner was in full swing with the dinner crowd. Kyle scanned the room, looking for Dorthea and Bea. Jack was just behind him. "You okay? You seem a little on edge."

"Me? I'm fine. Why?"

"You look nervous."

"Not me. I'm cool as a cucumber."

A young woman in a blue smock greeted them. "You looking for Lauren, Sheriff? She's off tonight."

"Not this time, Isabel. We're looking for Dorthea and Bea."

Isabel nodded toward the rear of the dining area. "They're back there." She turned to the man standing next to Kyle. "Can I get you anything, Mister...?"

"Pearce. Jack Pearce. Detective."

"Oh, a detective." She smiled.

"From Chicago," Kyle interjected.

"Okay, I'm no longer impressed." Isabel winked at him.

Jack smiled.

"Come on." Kyle led the way to the rear of the diner, where Bea and Dorthea sat, enjoying their dinner.

"I kid you not," Bea was saying. "I saw them holding hands in the back of the flower shop!"

"You did not!" Dorthea exclaimed. "By the carnations?"

"By the carnations!"

"Good evening, ladies," Kyle said.

They looked up from their meals and smiled at their visitors.

"To what do we owe the pleasure, Sheriff?" Bea asked.

"Bea," Kyle said, "You know I'm not the sheriff. I'm only filling in until they find my dad's replacement."

Bea looked him over, hat to shoes. "Well, you get *my* vote," she said.

"Thank you. That's very kind." He didn't want to continue with that topic. "Would you mind answering a few questions? We're trying to confirm some information, and we think you might be able help."

Dorthea looked up from her plate of chicken cordon bleu. "Oh, an interrogation!"

"Will there be handcuffs involved?" asked Bea. She looked past Kyle, finally noticing the stranger behind him. "And who's this handsome fellow?"

Jack held out his hand. Bea took it. Jack bent and placed a gentle kiss on the back of hers. "Jack," he said. "Pleased to meet you."

Bea shuddered. "Single, I hope?"

Dorthea reached across the table and slapped Bea on the arm. "He's young enough to be your son!"

"I know. He's perfect."

Jack smiled again.

"Two nights ago, you had dinner with Beverly," Kyle said.

Dorthea looked confused. "We did?"

Bea's face turned serious. She shot Dorthea a look. "Yes, we did. *Remember?*"

Dorthea met Bea's gaze. "Oh yes! We did! We were here at the diner!"

"Hannigan's!" Bea shouted. "We ate dinner at Hannigan's!"

Jack and Kyle exchanged glances. "Which was it?" Jack asked.

"Hannigan's," Bea said.

"The diner," Dorthea said.

Kyle looked from one to the other, then back again. "Lying to a law enforcement officer is cause to get you arrested."

Bea and Dorthea looked at each other again. Bea shook her head in warning. Dorthea looked up at Kyle.

"Dorthea, don't," Bea said.

Dorthea glared at Bea. "I have to! I can't go to jail! Do you know what they do to pretty people like me in jail?"

"Please!" Bea exclaimed. "You're older than I am, and I know for a fact that you haven't seen any action since the Reagan administration!"

"Dorthea?" Kyle said.

Dorthea set her napkin on the table, then neatly folded it. She picked up the fork and pushed her chicken around on the plate.

"Dorthea?" Kyle repeated.

Dorthea laid the fork on the plate and looked straight at Bea. "She wasn't with us."

"DORTHEA!" Bea yelled loud enough that everyone in the diner turned to look at them.

Kyle sighed. "Do you know where she was?"

"No," Bea said.

"Yes," Dorthea said.

"Dorthea," Kyle sighed, "Where was Beverly two nights ago?"

Dorthea took a breath. "She was with Mayor Hawthorne."

"The mayor?" Jack said.

"Thank you, Dorthea," Kyle said. He turned to leave.

Bea reached up and touched Kyle's arm. "Wait. What about the handcuffs?"

17

Saturday, September 22, 1990

3:46 AM.

Kyle stared at the red numbers on the clock and willed them to change.

He'd awoken from a disturbing dream and couldn't get back to sleep. As he lay there, he counted the seconds until the next minute.

Three, two, one.

3:47 AM.

He rolled over, shut his eyes, and tried to drown out the thoughts that were running through his head, but the silence of the house was deafening.

His latest dream crept back in: He was in the middle of a lake in a small rowboat that he and his dad had built one summer. His dad was sitting next to him, facing away, and they both had fishing poles with lines in the water.

Kyle's pole dipped, and the reel clicked as it spun out. He grabbed the pole and yanked, hooking whatever aquatic creature was on the other end of the line. The fish fought back with every inch, but he managed to bring it into the boat. Grabbing it by its mouth, he lifted it high into the air as if he were showing a trophy to a crowd.

When he turned to show it to his dad, he saw that the seat was empty. He scanned the surface of the water, looking for ripples, thinking his dad might have fallen in, but the water was calm. The only thing he saw were the clouds reflecting off the water's surface.

He glanced at the clock in time to see the numbers change.

3:49 AM.

It was Saturday. He should have been sleeping in, but as usual, nothing went as planned.

He shifted to his back and pulled the blanket up over his head. Fifteen minutes later, after finding a comfortable position, he felt himself drifting off.

His eyes opened, and he felt refreshed and fully awake. After tossing and turning all night, he was glad to have fallen asleep and stayed asleep long enough to get some much-needed rest. He rolled onto his side to check the clock. It must be close to eight or nine o'clock by now.

4:04 AM.

Oh, for fuck's sake!

He pushed the blanket to the other side of the bed and sat up. If he couldn't sleep, there was no need for him to keep trying. He found his way to the bathroom in the dark and turned the knobs to the shower.

18

Erica was cleaning up after breakfast. Otis had made omelets with diced tomatoes, onion, sausage, and bacon. It was the second-best meal she'd had in the past week. She dried the last plate and set it on the counter next to the other one, then folded the small hand towel and draped it over the back of a nearby chair. She glanced around the cabin.

Otis had gone to town for supplies. He hadn't been expecting company, and his refrigerator was looking bare.

A row of picture frames that were lined up on the fireplace mantle caught her eye, and she crossed the room for a better look. The first one was of a group of kids in little league jerseys. She picked it up, drawn to the scrawny girl in the front row with short hair and a filthy uniform. It was her. To little Erica's left was a boy, all skin and bones, his arm around little Erica's shoulder.

"Floyd." She touched the boy's face and smiled.

All the parents were in the back row, standing taller than the kids. She recognized the faces but couldn't remember their names. But there, second from the right. She knew that one.

"Mom." Her mom had passed away several years ago. If it weren't for Keith, she would have left Chicago and come back home right then. But his job had kept her there, so she'd stayed.

Mr. Otis was just behind Floyd, his hands resting on his grandson's shoulders.

The other pictures were placed neatly side by side: She and Floyd, the summer Mr. Otis took them fishing in his little rowboat. Floyd was upset that she had caught the biggest fish that day. He was always so competitive. She was seven that year; Floyd at his high school graduation, proudly holding his diploma for all to see; another one of Floyd graduating from Military Officer Candidate School, then another of him standing next to a helicopter, with a few of his Army buddies. It looked like they were in a desert somewhere. He looked handsome in his army uniform.

There was a picture of Mr. Otis and his wife Ruth taken on their wedding day in 1938. Mr. Otis was so young, so handsome. Floyd was the spitting image of his grandfather.

After a drunk driver killed Ruth and Floyd's parents in '68, Mr. Otis had raised Floyd as his own. Floyd had been eight when it happened during the fishing trip. When they got back to the house, police cars had overrun Mr. Otis's driveway.

A few months later, Erica's parents divorced, and her mom moved them to Chicago to be with her new boyfriend.

The last photo was of Mr. Otis, holding a giant cardboard check in the amount of seven million dollars issued by the Ohio Lottery Commission, dated January 8, 1983.

"What in the world?"

She returned the first photo, picked up this one, and scrutinized every inch.

Is this real?

The sound of a car coming up the road grabbed her attention. She put back the photo, debated whether she should ask him about it, then headed to the front door and pulled it open.

A Millhaven sheriff's patrol car was stopping in the dirt driveway. Erica froze. She wanted to run, but her feet wouldn't move. She watched as a middle-aged man with thinning white hair stepped out of the car and took a few steps toward her.

"Hello," the deputy said.

"Uh, hi." Her palms started to sweat.

The deputy kept approaching. "I'm looking for Otis. Is he here, by chance? I see his truck is gone."

"No. He went into town."

The deputy stopped. "I don't think we've met. I'm Leo. Leo Starke." He paused. "And you are?"

"I'm..."

I can't give him my real name.

"Jennifer."

"You a friend of Otis, Jennifer?"

Think of something quick.

"Family friend. He and my mom knew each other. I just arrived last night to let him know that she passed away last week."

"Oh, I'm sorry for your loss, ma'am."

"Thank you."

Leo nodded. "Do you know when Otis might be back?"

"I really don't. Do you want me to tell him you stopped by?"

"I'd appreciate that." He took a step backward. "And I'm very sorry about your mother. You have my condolences."

"Thank you."

Leo turned back to his car, opened the door, and dropped into the driver's seat.

She watched as he turned the car around in the driveway and waited until she could no longer hear the engine before she went back inside.

19

Kyle turned the Jeep onto the gravel road. Leaving the pavement behind, he twisted the knob next to the headlight switch and shifted the transmission into four-wheel drive.

About one-quarter mile into the forest, the gravel ended, and the road became dirt and rocks. The Jeep began to bounce and sway. He slowed to a crawl as the bumps got higher and the ruts got deeper.

Did something just scrape the bottom of the car?

He slowed even more.

It took forty-five minutes to reach his destination, weaving through the narrow forest and crossing through two shallow streams, but as soon as the trees parted and the 'road' smoothed into a grassy field, he knew it was worth it. It always was.

He stopped at the top of the mountain and gazed out over the treetops. The morning sky was a combination of blue and pink as the sun rose in the distance. Far below, nestled between the two mountain ranges, the town of Millhaven was waking up.

A few miles away, an eagle soared above the treetops, searching for its morning meal.

Seeing everything like this, from above cloud level, was serene. Majestic. He got out of the Jeep and strolled to the edge of the field. The air was crisp up here. He couldn't explain it, but it *tasted* different.

The journey of five miles begins with a single step.

Leaving the Jeep behind, he started on his weekly run.

The trail winded down the side of the mountain for half a mile before leveling out. From there, it snaked back up, passed through the forest, and finally, back to the grass field. He'd been running this circuit every Saturday morning for the past three years, weather permitting. It was difficult at first, but now he could run the entire five miles in under an hour, obstacles and all.

Some days, though, like today, the course afforded him time to think. This morning, he started at a brisk walk to warm up.

The topic foremost in his mind was the missing girl.

What happened at the Inn? What were Beverly and Mayor Hawthorne hiding that she had to lie about where she was that night and who she was with? And why was a detective from Chicago following me around, butting into my investigation, when a simple phone call would have sufficed?

He leaped over a fallen log.

That man I found in the woods. How did he get there? Who pushed him through that window? Did that same person shoot him? Or is there a third party involved?

There was a patch of dew-covered grass in his path. He matched his stride to avoid stepping in it. The last thing he needed was to slip and fall out here.

He reached up and pressed two fingers against his carotid, feeling his pulse. It was right where it should be for this amount of exercise. He sped up a little.

I need to check out that car. I'll do that this afternoon. Maybe get Leo to meet me at Andy's. Two sets of eyes are better than one.

The path inclined and twisted slightly to the right, and he felt his calves tingle. He picked up his pace a little more.

And where the hell is my patrol car?

Without realizing, he'd reached a full-blown run. He held that speed as he ducked under a fallen tree branch and hopped over a small boulder. His breathing was getting heavier.

He slowed to catch his breath, then stopped, leaned over, and put his hands on his knees. *Must be a storm heading this way. It's a little difficult to breathe this morning.*

His eyesight began to darken, and he felt a little dizzy. He reached out and leaned against a tree to steady himself. He grabbed for the water bottle that should have been clipped to his belt.

Damn. Must have left it in the Jeep.

He glanced up. Past the mountain range to the south, the sky was turning dark.

He took a few slow, deep breaths and could feel his heartbeat slowing.

He walked the rest of the way. *Take my time, listen to the birds sing their songs, try not to die.*

20

Serena did her best to maneuver her Volkswagen Cabriolet around the potholes on the narrow dirt road, but it was impossible to miss all of them. She pulled the seatbelt a little tighter.

The trees on either side of the road spread out to reveal a two-acre lot with a circular driveway and a double-wide trailer on the far side.

She pulled to a stop next to a blue Nissan Sentra. Before she could shift into park, a woman wearing a light blue and white waitress uniform emerged from the trailer. She gave Serena a quizzical look.

"Deputy Rios."

Serena had her windows down, enjoying the cool breeze. "Hi, Annie. Please, it's Serena. I'm off duty."

"Serena. What brings you out here?" She pulled a bobby pin from her shirt pocket and clipped a lock of curly blonde hair over her ear.

"I'm looking for Wes and Arnie. Are they here?"

"What did they do this time?"

"One of our patrol cars is missing. I want to see if they know anything about it."

Annie sighed. She reached into her purse and fished out her car keys. "Again?" She took a breath. "Try their 'camp.'" She motioned with her head toward a path in the trees. "Just over there, through the trees. The clearing isn't far. Should I be worried?"

"That depends on what they have to say."

"If they had anything to do with it, just lock them up. I'll come get them when my shift is over."

Serena looked at her, her head cocked to the side.

"At least I'll know they ain't getting into trouble."

She chuckled. "Thanks, Annie." She shut the car off, got out, and found the entrance to the path easily. As she neared the camp, she heard laughter and shouting. She stopped just inside the clearing.

On the far side, Arnie and Wes were spray painting their names on the side of a mud-covered car in bright, DayGlo pink. They were both covered in the same mud that was on the car. From her vantage point, she could see that at least one tire was flat, and the rear passenger window was shattered.

That's definitely Kyle's car.

As she approached, the taller of the two boys noticed her, grabbed the smaller boy's arm, and pointed in her direction. They both dropped their paint cans and ran.

"I know where you live!" she shouted.

They stopped and turned to face her.

"Here." She pointed to the ground in front of her. "Now!"

The boys moved toward her, watching their feet the whole way.

She looked past the boys to the car and noticed that, along with the flat tire and broken window, the light bar from the roof was missing, and the windshield was cracked.

"Explain."

"W-w-we found it," Arnie said. He reached up and brushed a lock of dirty blonde hair from his face.

"You found it? Where?"

"Out by the sign on Route 34," Wes answered. He mimicked his brother and ran his fingers through his hair. Where Arnie resembled their mom, Wes took after their dad, from his brown hair to his stocky linebacker build. And although Wes was a few years younger, he stood a good ten inches taller than his brother.

"Did it look like that when you found it?"

"N-n-no." Arnie glanced up at Wes, grinning. "It got b-b-broke on the way here."

"And just how, exactly, did it get here?"

The boys looked at each other.

"I kind of, maybe, drove it here?" Wes looked away from her.

"You drove it."

"It was just sitting there on the side of the road," Wes said. "The keys were in it, so we took it."

"W-w-we had to break the window to get in. It was l-l-locked."

Wes elbowed Arnie in the ribs. Arnie winced and exaggerated the action by doubling over as if in pain. "Don't tell her that, idiot!" He squared up to Serena and looked her straight in her eyes. "We want a lawyer."

"A lawyer?"

"Yeah, we got rights!"

She looked over her shoulder at the path that led back to her car and contemplated arresting them and putting them in the back seat. She just had it cleaned a few days ago, so she decided against that. "How old are you, Wes?"

"Thirteen."

"Arnie?"

"Sixteen."

She frowned at them, then glanced back at the police car and took a few steps toward it. An odor drifted toward her on the breeze, and she stopped. It wasn't just mud that was caked on the car. She covered her nose with the sleeve of her shirt. "Is that cow shit?" She peered inside the broken rear window, and something in the back seat caught her attention. She turned back to the boys. "Why is the back seat covered in feathers!?"

The boys exchanged glances, then burst out laughing.

21

Standing at the entrance of the three-story house, Kyle admired the detailed carvings of flowers and ivy on the large double doors. He pushed his finger into the doorbell and looked back at the driveway, admiring the dark gray Maserati parked outside of the four-car garage.

Being the mayor has its perks.

A few seconds passed before the door opened.

"Kyle! Come on in! What a pleasant surprise!"

"Mayor." Kyle shook the mayor's outstretched hand before following him inside.

"Armand, please. Let's go to the study." He led Kyle through the living room and into a slightly larger room. The bookcases lining every wall held a collection of first editions from various genres, from fiction and biographies to law references. Armand closed the sliding wood door and crossed the room to an oak desk. Beyond that, a large window overlooked the backyard and revealed a very impressive garden maze. In the distance, Kyle could see the boathouse and South Holston Lake.

"Please, have a seat." Armand slid into an oversized leather chair and scooted closer to the desk. Kyle lowered himself into one of the two smaller matching chairs across from him. "I'm glad you came."

"I'd like to ask you something of a sensitive nature."

Armand smiled, reached into the top drawer of his desk, and pulled out a large manilla envelope. He set it on the desk in front of him. "I've been wondering how long it would take."

"Sir?"

"For you to take over the business. Fill that gap that your father left." He slid the envelope toward Kyle.

Kyle was confused. "What's this?" He reached for the envelope. It was lumpy. It was heavy.

"Go on. Open it."

Kyle slid his finger under the flap and broke the seal on the package. Inside, he saw several stacks of one-hundred-dollar bills. He looked back up at Armand. "What is this?"

"That, my boy, is your cut."

"My cut? I don't understand."

Armand looked confused. "Yes, son. Your cut."

"My cut for what, exactly?"

Armand reached across the desk and retrieved the envelope. "I thought," he hesitated. "Why are you here?"

"I'm following up on my investigation." He leaned forward in the chair and nodded toward the envelope. "What's that for, exactly?"

Armand opened the top drawer of the desk and returned the envelope to its place. Kyle watched it the entire time. "What investigation?"

Kyle looked back at Armand, deciding to let that topic go for now. "Beverly said she was having dinner with Bea and Dorthea on Wednesday night. When I spoke with them, they said that she was with you. Can you confirm any of that?"

Armand's face showed a look of concern. "I'd like to ask for a little discretion." He folded his hands on the desk. "Mary..."

"Unless it's absolutely necessary, she doesn't need to know."

22

It seemed as if Armand was doing everything he could to avoid meeting Kyle's gaze. His eyes darted from the chandelier to the bookcase across the room, then he picked up a pen from his desk and rolled it between his fingers. Finally, he returned his attention to Kyle. "Yes. I was with Beverly that night. We had dinner at that steakhouse in Bristol."

Kyle nodded. "Bristol. Are you two…?"

"As I said, discretion."

"How long?"

He looked away. "Almost a year."

Kyle pulled a piece of paper from his pocket, unfolded it, then handed it to Armand. "This is the woman who disappeared from the inn. Does she look familiar?"

Armand took the paper, and his face turned white. His hands trembled.

"Armand?"

"Are you sure this is the missing woman?"

Kyle nodded. "Beverly confirmed it."

"Beverly." Armand's gaze never left the photo. "Yes, of course, she would have seen her. Would have talked to her." He shoved the paper back toward Kyle. "I have an appointment." He stood from the desk and motioned toward the door. "You should go."

Kyle stood. "Is everything okay?"

"Fine. Fine. It's an important meeting. I need to prepare."

Kyle turned and started toward the door. "About that envelope…"

Armand ushered Kyle forward. "We can discuss that at another time."

* * *

Kyle sat in his car, parked on the street at the end of the mayor's driveway, watching, waiting. He doubted that the mayor really had a meeting. In fact, he had the distinct impression that Armand just wanted him to leave. But why? There was no doubt that he had recognized the woman in the photo. Armand's reaction gave that away.

What's he hiding? And what was that envelope for? He said it was my cut. But my cut of what?

He couldn't see what was going on inside the house from this far away, but one thing was certain: after sitting there for forty-five minutes, the mayor was most certainly not expecting anyone.

His radio crackled, and Serena's voice called out. "Kyle, you there?"

He grabbed it from the seat next to him and pressed his thumb into the side button. "I'm here."

"Switch over to channel two."

He twisted the tiny knob on the top. "Go ahead."

"Hey, so I followed up with Annie Willis on your car."

He sighed. "Serena, it's our day off. Why are you working?"

"Okay, first, I have no life. You know that. Second, what are *you* doing right now?"

She has a point.

"Right," he said. "What did you find out?"

"Are you a good news first or a bad news first kind of person?"

"Serena."

"Okay, good news first. I found your patrol car."

He perked up, and his eyes grew wide. "That is good news. I assume the Willis boys had it?"

"Yeah… that's the bad news."

"Do I even want to know?"

"Probably not. Leo is taking them to the station as we speak. Annie wants us to hold them until she gets off work. But after you see the car, you might decide to keep them a bit longer. It's not a simple 'mom can pay the repair bill' kinda thing this time."

He tried to imagine what the car could look like.

"Whatever you're thinking, I guarantee it's worse."

"I'm about twenty minutes from the station. I'll meet you there."

"Copy that, Boss."

23

As Kyle approached the car, among the first things he noticed was the smell. It reminded him of summer on his grandfather's farm.

He surveyed the damage as he moved closer and, in his mind, worked out a rough estimate of what it might cost to bring it back into service. "Have Wes and Arnie admitted to causing the damage?"

"Yes," Serena answered. "And they were proud of it."

"Of course they were. Has Annie seen this yet?"

"No. She works late tonight. She probably won't get the chance until tomorrow morning."

Kyle stepped back and attempted to breathe in fresh air. He was unsuccessful. "That smell. Whose farm did they drive through?"

"They won't say."

"I'm sure we'll find out sooner or later. Someone's going to call and complain about car tracks in their field."

"I'm sure."

Someone coughed behind them. They turned to see Leo exit the station and head toward them, covering his mouth and nose with a handkerchief. "They're locked up all nice and tight."

"Gracias, Leo," Serena said.

He nodded, then got up close to her and whispered, "Thank you for making them wash up."

She grinned. "You're welcome."

Kyle went to the driver's side and pulled the door open. He saw that the dash cam was still intact. "Leo, can you pull that card? We should be able to piece together everything that happened to the car since I left Beverly's."

Leo frowned. "Me, Boss? You're right there."

Kyle scrutinized the interior. A breeze was flowing in through the broken window, causing the feathers from the back seat to drift into the front. They stuck to the drying mud on the seats, the dashboard, and the center console. He glanced up at Leo through the open passenger window. "I'm off duty."

Leo gave a sideways glance toward Serena.

She shrugged. "I'm off duty, too."

Leo shook his head. "Man..." He wrapped the handkerchief around his head, tied a simple knot, then leaned in through the window.

Kyle backed away from the car.

"What do you want to do with the boys?" Serena asked.

"They're both underage, and they don't have anything on their record yet." He noticed a spot of dirt on his shirt and wiped it off. "Let's let them simmer for a bit. Hold them until their mom picks them up."

She nodded.

"And see if we can make their stay so unforgettable that they won't want to come back."

"Copy that."

24

Otis was leaning on the counter, attempting the best he could to read the list of patients on the computer screen. The nurse glared up at him.

"Otis!"

He glanced away.

"I told you I'd help, but you need to stop." She shifted the glasses on her nose. There was a thin, gold chain wrapped from one stem to the other, hanging loose on the back of her neck. Her brown hair sat high on her head, tied into a bun. Her eyebrows raised as she looked at the screen through the bottom section of her bifocals. "What did you say his name was?"

"Keith."

"I don't see any Keith here. When did he come in?"

"'Bout two nights ago. Sheriff brought him in."

She read the names again. "Only one person was brought in two nights ago. A John Doe."

"Must be him. Any chance I can see him?"

She read some notes that were attached to the file. "I'm afraid not. He's still in recovery. He was shot up pretty bad, on top of all those broken bones."

"Will he be okay?"

"Doctors think so, but it's too early to tell." She looked up at him over the top of her glasses. "You said his name is Keith?"

"Thank you, Marlene. You're a doll." He turned and headed toward the exit.

He crossed the parking lot to his truck and slid behind the wheel, not noticing that he was being followed.

"Ooohh-we!" the stranger called out. "That is one sweet ride! What year is it?"

Otis looked up through the open door and smiled at the stranger. "1947."

"'47!? She's in great shape to be so old." The man stepped closer and ran his hand over the curve of the hood. "What's under here?"

Otis turned the key, and the truck rumbled to life. "All stock. 351 with aluminum intake, dual four-barrel carbs." He revved the engine for effect.

"Damn, listen to that thing growl!"

"Had it restored to fact'ry a few years back."

"I love it!" The man took his time as he went to the back of the truck, where he seemingly admired the wood-inlaid floor of the bed. The exhaust was letting out a low grumble.

"Thank you, sir, for your service." He came back to the driver's door and held out his hand.

"Come again?"

"Your license plate. World War Two veteran?"

Otis grasped the offered hand. "Yes, sir. Army Airborne. 82nd. I'd do it again in a heartbeat if I were thirty years younger."

The man nodded. "I'll let you get on with your day. You take care."

"You too." Otis closed the door and guided the truck out of the lot. Through the rearview, he saw the man watching as he turned onto the main road. "No, sir. That's not creepy. Not one bit."

25

Kyle was sitting behind his desk, with Serena next to him. They had been reviewing the dashcam footage on his computer, and it was paused on a close-up view of a henhouse mere inches from the front bumper. "That was the duty nurse at the hospital," he said.

"Oh?"

"She said Otis just came in and identified our John Doe."

"Otis?" Serena leaned forward in the chair.

"She said he called him Keith."

"Keith." She glanced back at the screen. "Well, that's a start."

He stroked his cheek with his knuckles. "I'm thinking maybe we should pay him a visit and see what else he knows."

She nodded.

He stood.

"Wait, now?" She looked up at him. "What about the rest of the video?"

"You don't have to go. In fact, you should go home. It's Saturday. Do whatever it is you do on your days off."

"No, no." She rose and followed him to the door. "I have absolutely nothing else to do today."

As they passed through the office, Kyle waved to Leo. "Leo, we're headed to Otis's to follow up on a lead. If I don't see you again this weekend, stay safe."

"Thanks, Boss! You too. See you Monday."

Serena hesitated. "Hang on. I almost forgot." She crossed the room to her desk, grabbed a copy of Jane's photo, and handed it to Leo. "This is the missing woman from Beverly's. Keep an eye out for her."

"Actually, I've seen her."

Kyle looked over at him.

"I drove out to Otis's this morning on my patrol, and she was there."

"She was at Otis's?" Kyle asked.

Leo nodded. "She told me her name was Jennifer."

"Jennifer," Kyle said. "Interesting. Did she say anything else?"

"Just that her mom was a friend of Otis's, that she'd passed away last week. She said she just got in last night and was planning on staying a few days."

Kyle's head cocked to the side. "Otis knows our John Doe *and* this missing woman? That can't be a coincidence."

"I agree," Serena said.

Kyle pulled his hat from the rack next to the door. "Leo, grab your keys and follow us out there, would you? We need to have a little chat with Jane. See if we can figure out what the hell is going on around here."

"Jennifer," Leo said.

"Melissa," Serena offered.

Kyle shook his head and pulled the door open.

26

Erica tugged the zipper of her gray jacket and flipped the hood up over her head. She pushed the cylinder of the revolver open and dumped the rounds into her hand. Four of the shell casings were empty. She placed those into her pocket, then loaded the other two back into the gun, staggering them so there would be one empty chamber between them. She tucked the gun into her waistband and stepped out into the brisk mid-morning air.

She paused on the porch and took in the scenery: the house was surrounded by the forest. The only way in or out of this little one-acre clearing was the dirt road to the left. The mountain rose behind the house with a steep incline.

It had been two hours since that cop left. Her nerves had settled, but she needed to clear her head and plan her next steps. She couldn't stay here with Mr. Otis. That would put him in danger, too.

She walked around to the left side of the house, toward the garage. Behind that, she could see the treehouse that she and Floyd had built so long ago. A few floorboards were missing, but the walls and roof still looked solid enough.

As she got closer to the garage, she noticed a shiny padlock on the doors. She gave it a tug, but it didn't budge. She wiped her sleeve on the small square window, removing years of built-up dirt, and peered through the glass. Inside appeared to be a car covered by a brown tarp. She couldn't tell what it was.

She made her way to the now grown-over path that she and Floyd used to take to the river. It took some doing, but she finally managed to move a small tree that blocked its entrance.

As she navigated the overgrowth, her thoughts turned toward

Keith. Otis was probably there now, at the hospital, trying to get whatever information he could. The main thing she wanted to know was if he was still alive. Once she knew that, she could start planning her next move.

The ground sloped upward even more. It'd been so long since she had navigated mountain terrain, and her legs reminded her of that with each step. A thorny vine latched onto her jacket, and she tugged it free.

After walking for what seemed like forever, she finally reached her destination: a large hollow tree stump.

She located a thick, dead branch and shoved it into the ground beside a large root. Pulling the branch toward her, she removed the top layer of grass and moss. She continued digging until she heard a faint thud.

Dropping to her knees, she dug her fingers into the ground and wrestled the Strawberry Shortcake lunchbox free from the dirt. It had seen better days: the paint was faded, and some spots showed a little rust. One side of the pink handle was broken.

She thumbed the rusty aluminum latch on the top and opened the lid.

27

"Erica?" Otis called out. He set the last paper bag of groceries on the table. The breakfast dishes from this morning were clean and were drying on the counter. "Erica?"

He checked the guest room, the main bedroom, then the bathroom. Except for him, the house was empty.

She must've gone for a walk.

He returned to the kitchen and started putting everything away.

Movement outside the window caught his attention: a blue sedan was driving up the road. He placed a glass jar of milk into the refrigerator, returned to the window, and pulled the sheer yellow curtain to the side.

Who's this?

The car came to a stop next to his truck, and he could see the driver.

That's the man from the hospital.

He grabbed the shotgun leaning against the wall by the front door, stepped onto the porch, and waited as the man climbed out of the car and started toward the house.

"I hope that's not for me."

"Depends," Otis answered. "Why you here?"

The man slowly reached into his back pocket and pulled out a wallet. He let it flop open, and a gold badge glimmered in the sunlight. "I'm Detective Jack Pearce, Chicago PD."

Otis recalled Erica's story.

Chicago. Is this the man who's chasing her?

"You a long way from home."

"I am."

Otis eyed him, attempting to size him up. "You didn't answer me.

Why you here?"

"I heard you talking to that nurse back at the hospital."

"Eavesdroppin'. That's a bad habit."

"Yeah, sorry about that." Jack returned the wallet. "Couldn't be helped. I heard you refer to that John Doe by his name."

"What of it?"

Jack took a step forward. "Thing is, that John Doe… Keith… is a prime suspect in my investigation."

"That right?"

"That's right."

"And what is it you investigatin'?"

"I've been tracking a fugitive."

Otis paused. "What's that got to do with me?"

"I was wondering," Jack took another step. "How do you know Keith?"

"That's none of your business."

Jack drew his gun from its holster and leveled it at Otis. "Why don't you place that shotgun on the ground and take a step back? Then, you and me can go inside and have a little chat, all friendly like."

Otis took a breath. He felt the weight of the shotgun in his hands. "I have another idea." He raised the weapon and pointed it at Jack. "Why don't you get off my property, and I let you live?"

Jack cocked the hammer on the revolver. "I'm giving you a lawful order to drop that weapon."

"In case you forget, you ain't in Chicago. You ain't got no authority here. Right now, you just trespassin'."

"I'm not gonna tell you again, old man."

"That's funny. I was about to say the same thing to you."

Jack pulled the trigger, and the revolver bucked. Otis's instincts took hold, and he reflexively fired a volley of double-aught buck, then sidestepped to his left. He pulled the fore end of the shotgun to the rear, ejecting the spent shell, then pushed it forward again, loading another round into the barrel. He dropped to his knee and took cover behind the post.

He didn't feel right. His side was burning.

He noticed a red stain slowly growing from a small hole in his shirt. "Shit."

That's gonna hurt.

Jack had retreated to the rear of his car and was hiding behind the trunk. He peeked over the vehicle. Otis fired another shot, bombarding the car with tiny lead pellets.

"Ain't tellin' you again! Get off my property!"

"I think we've passed that point, don't you?" Jack leaned around the car and blindly fired a shot back at Otis.

28

As Erica was making her way back toward the house, she heard the first shot, quickly followed by another. She dropped to the ground and listened.

Did that come from the house?

Otis!

She ran as fast as the forest let her, jumping over stumps and pulling herself free from the prickles. There was another gunshot, then another. They sounded like two different guns. One was definitely louder than the other.

Through the trees, she caught sight of the back of the garage. Then she saw the house. She pulled the revolver from her waistband and cautiously approached from the side. She sprinted the last few yards to the house, pressed her back against it, and peered around the corner.

There was a dark blue car in the driveway. She could see the top of someone's head behind the trunk. Suddenly, he popped up and fired a shot toward the front of the house, and she saw his face.

Jack.

She dropped into a crouch.

How does he keep finding me?

Another shot rang out, seemingly from right beside her. She glanced around the corner in time to see Otis rack the shotgun. "Otis!"

He looked over at her. "Child! Get out of here! Go!"

She looked from him to Jack, her mind attempting to devise a plan to get them both to safety.

"You!" Jack shouted. He fired at her, and the round hit the railing mere inches from her face. Wood shards splintered and flew into the air next to her head. She raised the revolver and squeezed off a shot.

The bullet found its mark and ripped through Jack's shoulder, and he fell backward.

"Otis, run!"

He didn't move; he just sat there and looked at her. She noticed the blood on his shirt and on the ground beneath him. He had dropped the shotgun and was now holding his side with both hands, covering the wound. "Listen," he said. His breathing was slow; his voice was gravelly. "Under the coffee table. Loose board. Get yourself safe."

She watched, helpless, as he grabbed the shotgun with one hand and the porch railing with the other, pulled himself up and leaned on the railing. He aimed the gun at Jack.

Jack fired through the sunflowers, and Otis fell onto his back.

"Otis!" She stepped out into the open, aimed the revolver, and squeezed the trigger. The round landed dead center of Jack's chest, and he stumbled, then fell backward. She kept pulling the trigger, resulting in clicking as the hammer fell on empty chambers and the cylinder rotated.

Realizing that the gun wasn't firing, she stopped and looked back at Otis. She couldn't tell if he was breathing.

She glanced over at Jack; he was leaning against the side of the car, pushing himself up. She watched as he pulled his shirt open and plucked the thirty-eight round from his ballistic vest. He held it up to examine it, then tossed it to the ground.

"Go!" Otis said.

She didn't move.

"Run!"

Without another thought, she turned and ran back into the forest.

29

Kyle swerved to avoid a pothole, and Serena grabbed the handle above the passenger door to brace herself.

She looked in the side mirror in time to see Leo hit the same hole. The patrol car bounced a few times as it recovered. "That had to hurt."

He looked back in the rear-view. "We should really look into getting four-wheel drives."

"That would be awesome," she glanced over at him. "As long as someone would stop losing our cars."

He shot her a sideways glance. "Funny."

She smiled. The Jeep hit a large rock in the road, causing her to hit her head against the roof. "OW!" She glared at him. "Mierda! You did that on purpose!"

"Prove it."

There was a bang from somewhere nearby.

"Was that a gunshot?" she asked.

"Probably hunters."

Turning the last corner, they saw Jack's car parked next to Otis's truck. Jack was standing on the porch, a gun in his hand.

He hit the brakes and pushed the gear lever into park. Erica was out of the car before it stopped sliding on the dirt driveway. He was right behind her. They drew their weapons as they sprinted the short distance to the house.

"What's going on?" Kyle yelled. As he climbed the steps, he saw Otis lying with his back propped against the railing. "Otis!" He holstered his gun, fell to his knees, and pressed his hands against the wound in his side.

Serena was already on the radio, calling for an ambulance. She scanned the forest, looking for any threats.

Leo joined her, and the two of them encircled the house, checking the treehouse and looking through the windows of the locked garage.

"Clear," she reported. "Moving inside."

"What happened?" Kyle asked. He was still holding Otis's wound. Jack appeared to be in shock. "Jack. Holster your weapon."

Jack did as he was told and slid the revolver into its holster.

"What happened?" He asked again.

"I don't know. He started shooting as soon as I got out of the car."

Kyle surveyed their surroundings, looking for any potential hostiles. Everything was still and quiet. The only sounds were Serena and Leo moving around inside the house. He noticed Jack's wound. "Your arm."

Jack looked down at his shoulder and saw a small hole in his shirt. Blood was trickling from it. "I'm fine."

"You're not fine, you're shot!"

"Ambulance is ten minutes away," Serena said as she passed through the front door, Leo two steps behind.

"House is clear," Leo said.

"We don't have ten minutes." Kyle reached around Otis's torso and leaned him forward. "Leo, give me a hand."

Leo grabbed Otis's legs, and together, they lifted him. Serena ran ahead and opened the back door of Leo's cruiser, then jogged around to the other side. Kyle laid Otis on the seat.

Serena reached through the car, grabbed Otis under the arms, and pulled him the rest of the way in.

Kyle climbed in and shut the door. "Serena, call EMS and tell them we're headed their way. We'll meet them on the road."

"Copy."

"And get Jack into the Jeep and follow us."

She nodded, slammed the car door shut, then ran back toward the house. Jack was descending the stairs. He fumbled on the first step and fell, reaching for the railing. He missed, and Serena grabbed his arm in time to keep him from hitting his head on it.

"I got you." She steadied him, helped him to the Jeep, then eased him into the passenger seat. She fastened the seatbelt around him.

30

Erica had found the loose boards under the coffee table, where Otis said they were. She stood above the hole in the floor, looking down at two old, faded green, metal ammo boxes.

She kneeled, pulled them free from their hiding place, then took them to the dining room table. As she passed the open front door, she instinctively glanced at the porch, the last place she'd seen Otis. The small pool of blood was turning brown.

Is he alright?

She forced herself to look away and set the boxes on the kitchen table. The locking latches opened easily. Her eyes widened when she saw several stacks of twenty-dollar bills, all wrapped in purple banker's straps.

She removed each stack, one by one, and set them on the table. Between both boxes, there were thirty-four stacks. She did the math.

Two thousand dollars per stack, that's sixty-eight thousand dollars. Jesus, Otis.

She glanced at the photos on the mantle. Specifically, the one of Mr. Otis holding that lottery check.

I guess that answers that question.

She also found a Sig Sauer 9mm semi-automatic pistol in one box. She pulled it out and thumbed the little round button behind the trigger, and the magazine dropped into her hand. There were fifteen rounds of hollow point ammunition, plus another round in the chamber.

She pushed the magazine back into the pistol and slammed it home with her palm, then tucked the weapon into the back waistband of her jeans, and shoved two of the stacks of twenties into her back pockets.

The rest she returned the boxes.

After replacing the floorboards and moving the coffee table back into place, she headed for the door, grabbed Otis's keys from the hook on the wall, and made her way to the garage, where she set the boxes onto the ground. She then tried every key on the ring until she found the one that fit the padlock. She returned the keys to her pocket and tugged the door open. Dust flew everywhere as fresh air entered the room for the first time in God knows how long.

She reached down, grabbed the corner of the tarp covering the car, and lifted it high enough to see what was hiding underneath.

She had seen this car before, albeit in a much rougher shape. Mr. Otis had brought the 1969 Plymouth Barracuda home on the back of a tow truck one summer. He and Floyd were planning on rebuilding it.

What she saw now, however, looked like it belonged on a showroom floor. Where there had once been rust spots and holes, there was now a pristine yellow metal flake paint job with black stripes running down the sides. The dirty, ripped-up cloth seats were gone, replaced with brand-new, shiny black leather.

I can't really stay inconspicuous driving this thing around.

She also couldn't drive Mr. Otis's truck, since everyone in town would recognize that.

Jack's car, it is.

Shotgun pellets riddled the entire driver's side of the sedan, with the majority of them concentrated on the rear quarter panel. None of them looked like they had made it through to the other side, though, which meant that none of them had hit their target.

What a shame.

She pushed the button in the glove box, and the trunk popped open.

She grabbed the ammo boxes and set them inside. It took a few slams to finally latch the trunk lid shut; the pellets had broken the latch off, and it was hanging on with one bolt. Once she was certain it wouldn't come open again while she was driving, she pulled the driver's door open and slid in behind the wheel.

When will people learn to stop leaving their keys in the ignition?

31

"He's still in surgery," the nurse said. "If he makes it, it'll be a miracle."

"Thank you," Kyle said. "Please keep us updated."

She nodded, then pushed through the double doors behind her.

Serena turned to face him. "What the hell is going on?"

"I wish I knew." He surveyed the waiting room. "Where's Leo?"

"He's still with Jack."

"How is he?"

"Jack? He has a few stitches in his arm, but otherwise he's fine. The bullet grazed him."

"He got lucky."

"Very."

He saw the look of concern on her face. "You're worried."

"I'm confused. The doctor said the *bullet* grazed him."

He nodded. "I caught that, too. Otis had a shotgun."

She nodded. "Which was loaded with buckshot. So, where did the bullet come from?"

"There must have been someone else. A third shooter."

"Our Jane Doe, maybe? Jennifer"

He shrugged. "Maybe. Whatever happened, Detective Pearce isn't being completely honest with us."

"I agree. What should we do about it?"

"I'll handle him. One way or another, he's going to tell me the truth about why he's really here."

Something caught Serena's attention, and she motioned toward the entrance with her chin. "Looks like word got out."

Kyle turned and saw Eric, Bobby, and Ray enter.

"How should we handle this?" She asked.

"We tell them only what they need to know: There was an accident, and Otis is in surgery. We don't know anything else at this time."

She nodded. "I'll take care of it." She placed her hand on his arm for a brief instant. "We'll figure this out."

"I know."

She left him and intercepted the three men.

"Sheriff," the nurse called from behind the desk. Kyle moved closer. "You can see the detective now."

He followed as she led him through the halls to one of the patient rooms, where Jack was putting his shirt back on, careful not to disturb the fresh bandages on his shoulder. Kyle noticed that the one on his forearm had been changed as well. Leo was leaning against the window on the far side of the room, his arms crossed.

"Leo, can you give us a minute?"

"Sure thing, Boss. I'll be in the waiting room if you need me." He closed the door on his way out.

Kyle glared at Jack. "What the hell happened out there?"

Jack winced as he started buttoning the shirt. "Like I said before, I got out of the car, and he started shooting. I shot back."

"I'm not buying the self-defense routine. What were you doing there in the first place?"

"You're questioning me? You should be talking to the old man."

"He's still in surgery. They don't know if he's going to make it. So yes, I'm questioning you." He took a breath. "I'll ask you again: what happened?"

"Earlier today, I came to the hospital to check up on John Doe. The old man came in..."

"Otis."

"Otis came in and asked the nurse about John Doe. Said John's name was actually Keith. Otis bugged out in a hurry, and I followed to see if I could get some more information."

"You followed him?" Kyle started pacing. "To his house? Need I remind you that you're not a police officer in this town? Hell, not even in the state. You have no authority to conduct any investigations here." He stopped and looked back at Jack. "In Chicago, what happens when there's an officer-involved shooting?"

Jack looked confused. "Come again?"

"What's the procedure?"

"The officer is placed on administrative leave pending an investigation."

73

"What about a civilian-involved shooting?"

"The civilian is arrested, and detectives investigate."

"Until now, I've afforded you professional courtesy. But you're still just a visitor here. An average citizen. And I have to treat you as such." He reached into his back pocket and pulled out a pair of handcuffs.

"What are you doing, Sheriff?"

"Face the window and put your hands behind your back."

"You're arresting me? Under what charge?"

"Let's start with stalking, trespassing, aggravated assault with a deadly weapon, and attempted murder."

"Are you serious?"

"If Otis doesn't make it, I'll add first-degree murder to those charges."

"Sheriff," Jack said calmly. "You don't want to do this."

"You're right, I don't. But until I start getting some answers that make sense…"

He placed the cuffs around Jack's wrists and clicked them shut, then turned Jack to face him.

Jack was grinning.

"You have the right to remain silent."

32

Erica entered the hospital and went straight to the information desk. She kept her head low and avoided eye contact with everyone she passed.

The nurse behind the counter glanced up from the computer screen as she approached. "Good afternoon."

"Hi." She noticed a camera on the wall behind the nurse that was pointed down in her direction, and reached back, pulled the hood of her jacket up, and hid her face from its view. "I was hoping I could get some information on a couple of patients."

"Oh, of course." The nurse sat up and placed her hands on the keyboard. "Are you family?"

"Yes. One is my fiancé, Keith Peterson."

The nurse tapped her fingers on the keys and scrutinized the screen. "I'm sorry, I'm not seeing a Keith Peterson. What's the other name?"

"Otis. Otis Johnson."

She looked up from the monitor, eyebrows raised in concern. "Otis is still in surgery, dear, but you're welcome to wait with everyone else." She pointed to the waiting room behind Erica, to her left. She turned to follow her gaze and saw three men sitting under the window on the far side of the room. Standing next to them was Leo, the deputy she'd met earlier that morning, talking with a woman she didn't recognize.

Her stomach knotted. She couldn't breathe. She was turning back to the nurse when the double doors swung open, and Jack walked through, followed closely by the cop who had taken Keith. He was wearing civilian clothes now, but she recognized him as soon as she saw him.

She spun away and hid her face with her hand.

"You okay, Hun?" the nurse asked. "You look pale."

Erica's legs went limp, and every muscle in her body trembled. She leaned against the counter. "I'm fine."

"Kyle?" the woman behind her asked. "What's going on?"

"Is this the man who shot Otis?" One of the men asked.

Yes. Yes, it is.

"Who said anything about a shooting?" Kyle asked.

"Come on, Kyle, we ain't stupid!" Another of the men said.

Keeping her head low, she slowly looked over her shoulder.

The other two men nodded in unison. One of them pointed to another. "Besides, Bobby's got a police radio! We heard everything!"

"Shut up, stupid!" Bobby said. "You don't tell the cops you got a police radio!"

"Don't call me stupid, stupid!"

"Enough!" the woman said. "Where did you get a police radio?"

Bobby glared at his two companions and shook his head.

"From them Willis boys!" One of them blurted. "We got a nice roof light, too!"

Kyle rubbed his temples with his free hand and shook his head. He pushed Jack toward Leo. "Take Mr. Pearce here and find him a nice, cozy room in our jail. I'll be along shortly to do the paperwork."

"Yes, sir."

33

Erica watched in wonder as Leo took hold of Jack's arm and led him out of the hospital. She noticed that Jack's hands were bound behind his back.

She listened to their conversation.

"Kyle?" the woman said.

"Serena."

Serena. Is she a cop, too?

"Is this your way of handling things?"

"Have you heard anything back from Chicago?" He asked.

"Not yet."

"Get on the phone. Don't stop calling until you talk to someone."

Chicago? Call who? Are they talking about me or Jack?

The desk phone rang, and the nurse picked it up. Erica tuned her out until the nurse called out, "Sheriff? You have a phone call."

Kyle stepped up to the desk and took the receiver from her. "Deputy Lorne."

He was standing so close that she could smell his cologne.

"Okay. Thanks," he said. "I'll Be there shortly." He handed the phone back to the nurse and started for the exit. "Serena, I'll meet you at the station in a bit."

"Everything okay?" Serena asked.

"Yeah. I need to run an errand."

"An errand? Now?"

He pushed through the glass doors, then climbed into a green Jeep that was parked nearby, and drove away.

"Crap," she heard Serena say.

"Everything okay?" the nurse asked.

"I need a ride!" Serena sprinted out of the hospital.

Erica hadn't realized she'd been holding her breath until she let it out. Her head dropped to the counter, and she tapped her forehead against it several times.

Jesus, that was close.

The doors swished open, and she heard someone walking up behind her.

"I almost forgot," Serena said. Erica's heart stopped. "Can you call me when Otis is out of surgery?"

"Yes," the nurse said, "Of course."

"Thanks." She turned and exited back through the doors.

Erica glanced over her shoulder in time to see Serena get into the patrol car with Leo and...

Jack was staring in her direction.

Did he just wink at me?

She didn't relax until the patrol car left the parking lot. She turned back to the nurse. "Thank you."

The nurse nodded.

On her way to the exit, she passed the three men, still yelling at each other.

Outside, she paused, recalling their earlier conversation, and scanned the cars in the lot, looking for one in particular.

There.

She crossed the lot to a beat-up Ford Ranger with chipped white paint, mismatched wheels, and a police car emergency light shoved into the bed, nestled between a rusty car transmission and a stuffed deer head.

The tinted windows were down, giving her full access to everything inside, including a poorly wired police radio.

She reached in and pulled the radio from its homemade wooden mounting box. The wires, which were attached to the speakers by clear cellophane tape, broke apart easily.

She tucked the radio under her jacket and headed toward Jack's sedan, parked several blocks away behind an old church.

34

Serena stood nearby as Leo helped Jack from the back of the cruiser and guided him into the station. She followed closely behind.

"Hi, Bob." She said as the door closed behind her. Deputy Robert Parker was leaning back in the chair at his desk, reading the latest issue of *Field & Stream*. He lowered the magazine as she walked past.

"Hey, Serena. I see you brought me another guest."

She glanced toward the back hallway, toward the jail cells. Leo was walking Jack through the door at the end. "Yeah, Jack Pearce. He and Otis had some sort of... altercation. Kyle wants to keep an eye on him until he figures out what happened."

Bob put the magazine on his desk and leaned forward. "That's him? I heard it all over the radio. He okay?"

"He was still in surgery when we left the hospital."

"Jesus." Bob couldn't hide his look of concern.

"Yeah." She turned the corner into the holding area.

There were three cells along the exterior wall, each of them six foot by six foot. The Willis boys were in the cell farthest to the right. Leo took Jack to the one on the left, leaving the middle cell empty. He guided Jack into the cell, then closed the door behind him. It latched with a loud clang.

"It's about time," Wes said.

"Yeah! We've been in here all d-d-day! I have to p-p-pee!"

"Pipe down, you two. Your mom should be here soon." Leo turned his attention back to Jack. "Hands."

Jack turned, faced the far wall, and backed up to the door. Leo unlocked the handcuffs through the bars and removed them from Jack's wrists.

"When do I get my phone call?"

"When Kyle gets back." Leo glanced at his watch. "Should be a couple of hours."

Satisfied that he was securely locked inside his new home, Serena returned to her desk. She had just lowered herself into her chair when the front door opened, and Annie Willis strolled in.

"Hi, Annie. You here for the boys?"

"That depends. How bad is the car?"

"It's bad. Probably a total loss. The insurance company will be here Monday to take a look."

"That's just great. How am I gonna pay for that?"

Serena rose from the chair and walked toward the holding area. "I was thinking about that. What do you think about having the two of them work it off?"

"You mean, like, community service or something?"

"Yeah, something like that. I'm sure we can find something for them to do."

"I like that. It'll keep them busy while I'm at work, and it just might teach them that their actions have consequences."

"I'll have to talk with Kyle and see if I can get him on board."

"You think he'll do it?"

"I don't see why not. They can come by after school, and you can pick them up on your way home."

Annie smiled. "If Kyle agrees."

"If Kyle agrees. I'll be right back."

Annie sat in one of the wooden chairs along the wall and placed her purse in her lap.

35

"Okay, boys," Serena said, "Your mom's here. Time to go."

"N-N-NO! We want to stay!"

"You can't make us leave!"

"P-p-*please*! She'll spank us!"

She unlocked the cell and tugged the door open.

Wes' head dropped, and his shoulders sagged. "Fine. Come on, Arnie. Let's go face the music."

Arnie slowly exited behind Wes. "M-m-mom's music sucks."

Serena smiled and led them to the front of the station.

Annie stood when she saw the boys. "What's all this?" She reached out and combed her fingers through Arnie's hair.

"M-m-mom, stop!"

"I made them wash up before we brought them in," Serena said. "Couldn't have them messing up my jail."

Annie smiled. "You're gonna have to tell me how you did that. It's nothing short of a war when I try to get them to clean up."

She eyed the boys. "We came to an understanding, didn't we?"

Wes met her gaze for the briefest of instances. "She threatened to use a switch on us if we didn't."

"Yeah, it was police b-b-brutality."

"Keep talking," Serena said. "I'll show you police brutality."

Annie corralled the boys out of the station. "Let's go. You still have that mess in the kitchen you need to clean up from yesterday."

"Mom!"

"Don't 'mom' me. You know the rules. You made it, you clean it."

Serena's desk phone rang. She crossed the room and lifted the receiver to her ear. "Deputy Rios."

"Deputy Rios, this is Captain Frank Marshall, Chicago police, ninth district." The voice was gravelly, as if he'd been a smoker for the majority of his life. "I hear you've been trying to reach me."

"Yes, sir, I have. It's about one of your detectives. Jack Pearce?"

The line was silent for a moment. "Yes?"

"We just want to verify that he's with your department and he's here on official business."

Captain Marshall hesitated. "Is this some sort of joke, Deputy?"

This caught her off guard. "I'm sorry?"

"You should be. If you're trying to be funny, you've got a lot to learn about humor."

"Sir, I mean no disrespect, and I apologize if I offended you." She took a breath. "There's a man here who says he's a detective with your district. We're just trying to get some background on him."

"Deputy... what's your first name?"

"Serena, sir."

"Serena. Detective Pearce was shot and killed in the line of duty two years ago. I don't know who that person is, but he is *not* Detective Jack Pearce."

36

Erica closed the trunk of the 1979 AMC Concord and eyed the rust spots, which, oddly enough, closely matched the faded brown paint.

She dug a dime from her pocket and used it to remove the screws that were holding the rear license plate to the car and replaced it with the one she'd taken from another car.

She crossed the lot to the entrance of the motel, tossing the old plate into a dumpster as she passed.

The decor of the lobby screamed 1960s: red walls with orange curtains, red vinyl furniture, and a yellow shag carpet. The room smelled of stale cigarettes.

She cautiously approached the desk and noticed that the man behind the counter smelled of body odor and cheap liquor. The top five buttons of his shirt were undone - or were they missing? She couldn't tell. His thinning hair was meticulously combed over a bald spot and held in place by what appeared to be industrial-strength hairspray, and he wore a single thick gold chain around his neck. When he smiled, she saw that two of his front teeth were missing, one on the top and one on the bottom.

"But I do offer a nice massage. Free of charge."

"Tempting, but I'll pass."

He frowned. "How many nights?"

That's a good question.

"How much for the rest of the month?"

"The whole month?" He pulled a calculator from under a stack of magazines and tapped its keys. "Three hundred seventy-five."

She pulled a wad of cash from her pocket, peeled off four one-hundred-dollar bills, then shoved the rest back. She handed him the fee. His eyes were glued to the stack of cash. "Keep the change."

He nodded as he held out a key attached to a yellow triangular keychain. "212. Second floor, back of the building."

"Thanks." As she turned to leave, he grabbed her wrist.

"You change your mind about that massage…"

"I know where to find you."

She found the room exactly where he said it would be.

As she closed the yellow-brown curtains, she turned toward the single-sized bed with its dull red covers and dumped the clothes she had bought at the flea market earlier this morning. Sifting through them, she folded each one before neatly placing them into the drawers of the worn-down dresser.

She kept replaying the events from the hospital, over and over, in her mind. Specifically, the conversation she'd overheard about Chicago and, more importantly, the local cops arresting Jack. She looked at the police radio she'd pulled from the pickup at the hospital. There were several wires, all of them different colors, poking out of the back.

How does this thing work?

37

Leo was sitting on the floor, leaning against the cell door. His head was twisted to the right and hung at an odd angle.

Kyle saw that his duty weapon and both spare magazines were missing. "Where were you when this went down?"

"I was in the men's room," Bob answered. He was standing in the doorway behind Kyle.

"You didn't hear anything?"

"Not a thing."

Kyle had seen dead bodies before; it came with the job. But this one was different. This one was his friend. He kneeled and examined Leo closer. "His keys are missing."

"So's his patrol car."

He glanced up at Bob, then Serena. She'd been watching him intently, writing notes in her notebook. He stood. "How did he get past you?"

Her eyes darted to the rear wall. "He went out the emergency exit."

"By the time we got back here," Bob said, "He was gone."

Kyle shook his head. "I want all hands on deck. Get Nathan and Betty in here. I want Jack Pearce back inside this cell before breakfast."

Bob nodded, then left the room. The two patiently waiting EMTs stepped aside to let him pass.

Kyle turned to Serena. "Did you get the photos?"

She tapped the camera that was hanging around her neck. "Yes."

He motioned to the EMTs, and they entered the room while he and Serena stepped out of their way. She grabbed his arm and steered him toward the front door.

"I spoke with Chicago."

He was only half listening, still focused on the back room.

"Kyle."

"Sorry. You spoke with Chicago. What did they say?"

"Detective Jack Pearce died two years ago."

"He died..." his mind was racing.

If that's true...

"Then who the hell's running around my town, shooting everything up?" He pushed the front door open and was greeted by a gathering crowd. News like this travels fast in small towns. They rushed toward him, and he motioned for them to stop. He looked back at Serena. "Let's get a perimeter set up. I want everyone back behind the parking lot."

"Copy that." She went back inside to gather the mobile barricades.

"Kyle, is it true?" someone shouted.

"Who was it?" came another voice.

He crept toward the crowd, ushering them backward, and they moved with him. "We'll let everyone know what's going on as soon as we can. Right now, we're still gathering information."

"Are we in danger?"

He tried to find the source of that last question: "We have no reason to believe that there's an immediate threat to anyone. We're..."

"Who was it?"

"Where is he?"

"What aren't you telling us?"

The questions were coming faster than he could answer.

"On your left," Serena said as she brushed past him, carrying an orange and white striped plastic sawhorse. She used it to nuzzle the crowd back to the parking lot entrance. "I need everyone to stay back here," her authoritative voice boomed above the dull roar of the crowd. "No one crosses this line, understood?"

The voices dropped to whispers as the crowd focused on the building. Kyle and Serena followed their gazes and saw the EMTs emerge from the station. One pushed a gurney from the rear; the other guided it from the front. A black, zipped-up, body-sized bag was strapped to it. Everyone stood in silence as the EMTs loaded the gurney into the back of the ambulance, closed the doors, and drove away.

A familiar voice called out: "Kyle."

He turned and followed the voice. "Lauren."

38

"Where is Deputy Lorne!?" Mayor Armand Hawthorne exited the station in a whirlwind, slamming the door against its frame.

Kyle met his eye as he and Lauren were walking toward the building.

Armand's face was red. "Inside, now!"

Kyle looked at him momentarily, taken aback by his sudden emergence, then back at Lauren. He smiled at her. "Can you wait for me? I'll just be a moment." She nodded. He motioned to Serena. "Would you mind sitting with her for a minute?"

"Of course." She guided Lauren to the waiting area inside the station.

Kyle went to his office, where Armand was pacing back and forth behind the desk. He thought he could see the veins in the mayor's forehead throbbing.

"What the hell is going on here, deputy!?"

It did not go unnoticed to Kyle that, for the first time since he'd taken charge of the department, Armand referred to him as 'deputy' and not 'sheriff.' He took a breath.

"Save it!" Armand cut him off. "In the last week alone, you've lost not one but two patrol cars. One of them was destroyed by two hooligans who aren't even old enough to drive!" He paused. "The second was stolen by the man who killed one of *my* deputies and escaped from *your* jail!"

"Sir…"

Armand's eyes snapped up at him. "This is *unacceptable!*" He stabbed his index finger on the desk for effect. He took a deep breath, crossed the room, and opened the office door. "Deputy Rios!"

Serena quickly entered the office and stood just inside the door.

Armand's hand was still on the doorknob. "Deputy Lorne is suspended and relieved of duty pending an investigation. Retrieve his badge and weapon, then escort him from the building."

Serena looked from the mayor to Kyle, then back to Armand. "Sir?"

"You're in charge now!" Armand left the room and turned down the hall toward the cells.

Serena faced Kyle. "Is he serious?"

He slid his gun from its holster and thumbed the magazine release. He set the magazine on the desk, then pulled the slide back and locked it open. He followed the round's trajectory as the ejector flung it into the air and guided his hand underneath it. The bullet landed in the center of his palm. He placed the round on the desk and handed her the empty weapon.

"Kyle."

"It's okay."

She pushed his hand away, not accepting the gun. "None of this is okay. He can't do this."

"He can." He offered her the gun again. "He did. Take it."

She hesitantly reached out, and he placed the gun in her hand. He pulled his badge from his pants pocket and set that on top of it.

She sighed. "What are you going to do?"

"Right now, I'm going to take Lauren home. Then, I suppose I'll stop by the hospital and check on Otis. See how he's doing."

"What about Jack? Are you just gonna let him get away? And Melissa – Jennifer – whatever her name is?"

He placed a hand on her arm and smiled at her. It was a warm, caring smile. "If anyone can figure this out, you can." He crossed the room and stepped through the doorway.

"You're just giving up?"

He turned back to face her. "You've got this."

"I'm not so sure about that."

39

Sunday, September 23, 1990

It was dark.

Otis heard a voice, unfamiliar and far away. He couldn't make out what it was saying.

"... hear me?" The voice was getting closer, clearer. It was a deep, slow voice, definitely male. "Mr. Johnson, can you hear me?"

He realized his eyes were closed.

His lids were heavy, and when he finally managed to open them, it took a few moments for his eyes to adjust to the bright light. Everything was out of focus, but he saw a large blue and white blur nearby.

"There you are." The blur leaned in closer, and Otis made out the shape of a man wearing a long white jacket over blue hospital scrubs.

He took two long, labored breaths that burned his lungs, which forced him to cough.

"It's okay. Take your time." The man pulled away, and he lost focus again.

"Mouth is dry," Otis said. His voice was raspy, his throat itchy.

The man retrieved a Styrofoam cup from a nearby stainless tray and maneuvered a straw to Otis's mouth.

He took a sip. "Thank you."

"How are you feeling?"

"You tell me." His throat stung from the cool drink. "Where am I?"

"You're in the hospital. You were shot. Do you remember that?"

"Shot. Yes. I remember."

"Good. That's good. Do you remember who shot you?"

Otis attempted to recall the event. "I was on my porch. There was a

89

car, a man."

"And a woman."

He nodded. "Erica."

"That's right. Erica. What else can you remember?"

"He said he was a cop. He said he was from…"

The man leaned in close again. Otis's eyes re-focused, and he recognized the man who had shot him. "It was you."

The heart rate monitor beside the bed beeped urgently as Otis's heart pounded. Jack reached up and pulled the wires from the bottom, and the machine went quiet. "Where is Erica, Mr. Johnson?"

Otis saw movement to his left.

"What's going on here?" A woman's voice called out.

A nurse?

Jack grabbed the stainless tray and crossed the room in two steps. He swung the tray and knocked it against the side of her head. As she fell to the floor, he turned back to Otis. "Where is she, old man?"

"Go to hell. Ain't' tellin' you nuthin'."

Jack pulled the pillow from under Otis's head and held it inches from his face. "We'll see about that."

40

Kyle had seen more of the hospital in the last two days than he ever wanted to. He slid his key ring into his pocket as he passed through the glass doors and was taken by surprise as a nurse in green scrubs ran through the lobby.

"Sheriff! Thank God you're here! Room 104!"

He informed her he wasn't the sheriff and no longer with the department, but she was already gone, having disappeared around a corner. Several other nurses emerged from a door on his right and followed closely behind her.

"What's going on?" He called out.

One of them stopped long enough to answer. "One of our patients and a nurse were attacked."

She had turned the corner on the other side of the room and was gone before he could respond.

He followed them into the hallway and turned the corner to find a nurse sitting in a chair against the wall, holding an ice pack against her head. One of her colleagues was standing over her, rubbing her back, while another kneeled beside her.

Several other nurses were packed into a room directly across from them, speaking in hushed voices. Kyle couldn't hear them or piece together what they were saying, but he could see that John Doe from the inn wasn't breathing, and the lines on the heart monitor weren't bouncing up and down like they should be.

"Sheriff," a raspy voice called out.

It was tired and weak, but he recognized it. "Otis." He turned to the room behind him, where Otis attempted to push himself up on the bed. He rushed to his side. "You shouldn't be sitting up."

"He's here, Sheriff."

"Who?"

"The man who shot me. That cop from Chicago. He's here."

Kyle's head swiveled, and he quickly scanned the room.

"He went that way." Otis was pointing down the hallway to the right.

"You alright?"

"I been worse. Go find that son of a bitch."

Kyle reached for the phone on the table next to the bed and dialed Serena's desk number.

She answered on the first ring. "Kyle, I was just about to call…"

He cut her off. "Serena, listen. I'm at the hospital. Jack attacked Otis, and I think he killed our John Doe. I need you guys down here."

He listened as she called out to Parker and Rogers. "We're on our way. Are you armed?"

He frowned. Usually, he would be, but she had his service weapon, and… "No, I never made it home. My personal is in my nightstand."

"Keep your head down. We'll be there in five."

41

Exactly four minutes and thirty seconds later, sirens blaring and lights flashing, Serena stopped the car just outside the emergency room. She reached over and unlatched the shotgun from its rack, then threw her shoulder into the door.

Kyle was waiting just inside. "I haven't seen him. Security has eyes on every exit." He pulled a two-way radio from his back pocket and showed it to her. "They'll call if they see him on camera anywhere in the building."

She nodded and handed him the shotgun. "You remember how to use this?"

He frowned. "Funny."

"Bob and Nathan are right behind me. Show me Otis's room. We'll start there."

He nodded and pulled the fore end of the shotgun rearward, opening the breach just enough to verify that there was a shotshell in the barrel.

She pulled her pistol from its holster and followed as he led her through the lobby.

"We've evacuated all non-essentials," Kyle said as they crossed the room. "There's us, the security team of five guards and a handful of nurses. And Esther finally gave birth this morning. She's on the second floor with her doctor, one additional nurse, and one guard."

"Esther? It's about freaking time. How many days past due was she?"

"Fourteen."

"Maldita. Are they armed?"

"Esther and the baby?"

She shot him a sideways glance. "The guards."

He grinned. "They are, but the shift supervisor said that they only shoot once a year when it's time for recertification."

She rolled her eyes. "Great."

When they entered Otis's room, a guard quickly turned and pointed his revolver at them.

Her instincts took over, and Serena brought her gun to bear and aimed her weapon at him. "Lower it."

The guard did as he was told. She nodded, then glanced over at Otis, who was sitting up in the bed. The white bandages on his chest and shoulder were turning pink.

"Don't stare so hard, missy," he said. "You'll make me blush."

"You okay?"

"I'm fine. You go catch that, what's the word I heard you say? Cabron?"

She smiled. "I'm working on it. Did he say anything to you?"

"No. He didn't say anything. I woke up, and I saw a nurse laying on the floor. He pulled those wires out," he nodded toward the heart monitor, "then came at me. Somethin spooked him, and he ran."

"Which way did he go?"

He pointed. "That way."

She turned back to the guard. "You stay here. Make sure nothing happens to him. Got it?"

"Yes, ma'am."

42

Erica ducked behind a metal shelf packed with neatly folded hospital scrubs.

Jesus, that was close.

She inched toward the door and peered through the window. There was a guard just a few feet away, facing away from her. His radio hissed, and he brought it to his ear. He nodded and said something that she couldn't hear, then she lost sight of him as he rounded the corner.

Her hands were shaking. She could feel her blood pressure rising.

She closed her eyes, took a deep breath, and counted to five.

"I don't believe it. God must love me."

Jack.

She turned and saw him coming down the hallway toward her. He was close enough that he grabbed her hair just as she turned to run.

"Where do you think you're going?" He tugged hard, and her head jerked backward. She felt his other arm wrap around her torso, and he pulled her in and held her tight.

"Let go of me!"

"Not this time."

She heard a faint metal click, then felt the cool steel of a blade press against her throat.

"Now, you're gonna tell me what I want to know. No more games, no more playing hide-and-seek."

She could feel his breath on the back of her neck.

"Where's that duffel bag you stole from me?"

"Ever hear of a breath mint?"

He tugged on her hair again, exposing her neck even more, and pressed the knife harder against it. "That's not nice."

"Neither is holding a knife to a girl's throat."

"Last chance. Where is it?"

She took a breath, and her muscles tensed up.

Now or never.

She squeezed her hand between his arm and her shoulder and slammed her foot down onto his with all her body weight.

His grip on her hair loosened enough for her to break free. Not wanting to lose the element of surprise, she spun and brought her knee up, planting it firmly between his legs.

He doubled over. She balled her hands into fists and slammed both down onto the top of his head, then ran full speed down the hallway, following the path the security guard had taken.

There was a stairwell on her right, and as she pushed through the door, she heard Jack cursing loudly behind her.

She closed the door, watching through the small glass window as he rounded the corner. She pressed her back to the wall.

43

Kyle turned the corner and saw him at the far end of the hall, peering through a small window in a door.

He leveled his shotgun. "Jack!"

Jack turned to face him. "Well, hello there, sheriff."

"On your knees. Hands behind your head."

Jack smiled. "Yeah. See, the thing is, that don't work for me." He took a step in his direction.

"That's far enough."

Jack lifted his hands and showed Kyle that they were empty. "I'm unarmed, Sheriff. You wouldn't shoot an unarmed man, would you?" He took another step forward.

Kyle moved backward, keeping his distance. "Last chance." He motioned toward the floor with the barrel of the shotgun.

"I was about to say the same thing to you."

Before Kyle could react, Jack had somehow closed the few feet between them and grabbed the shotgun with both hands. It was all Kyle could do to keep hold of it.

Jack pushed against the weapon, and the cold steel slammed into Kyle's face. He felt something warm and wet in his nose.

The next sensation he felt was a knee ramming into his kidney. He lost his grip on the shotgun, and fell to the floor. He found himself looking into the barrel of the 12-gauge. At the other end, Jack was smiling down at him.

"Can't say it's been fun," Jack said, "but it's definitely been interesting."

Kyle pressed a hand against his side as he tried to catch his breath. Attempting to ignore the pain, he stood. "You should give yourself up.

There's no way you're getting out of here." He noticed blood slowly seep from under Jack's shirt and trace its way down his arm.

His stitches must have ripped.

"Look, sheriff." He took a breath. "Do you mind if I call you Kyle?" He didn't wait for an answer. "Kyle, Leo pissed me off, and look what happened to him. Don't think for a second that I won't do the same thing to you."

"You really don't want to do that."

"No?"

"No."

"And why's that?"

Kyle jumped forward and grabbed the end of the barrel with both hands. He stepped to the side and pulled with all his strength.

This caught Jack by surprise, and he stumbled backward. Kyle wrestled the weapon away from him.

A volley of double-aught buckshot blasted a hole in one of the ceiling tiles above them.

44

Erica waited for the right moment.

Just a few more steps... NOW!

She flung the door open and jumped onto Jack's back, grabbed his head, and dug her fingers into his eyes.

He yelled as he grabbed at her wrists and tried to pull her hands away.

She wrapped her legs around his waist and yanked backward.

He lunged backward and slammed her into the wall. "Get the fuck off me!"

Kyle lashed out with the shotgun and slammed the butt of the weapon into Jack's stomach. He doubled over, and the added extra weight of a 145-pound woman on his back forced him to the floor. She rolled to the side and jumped out of the way.

Jack eyed them both as a sinister grin formed on his face. "Nice. You just saved me the trouble of chasing you." He pushed himself onto his knees. "Now I can kill you both and be done with it." He turned toward her and snarled. Blood covered his teeth and was seeping from the corners of his mouth.

"Shoot him," she said.

Kyle took a step forward. "Put your hands behind your head."

"Sheriff, shoot him."

"*Now.*"

Jack turned toward him. "You should listen to her, sheriff." He raised his arms and placed his hands on his head.

Kyle reached out and grasped one of his wrists. "I'm not the sheriff. Thanks to you, I'm not even a deputy."

"So, what you're saying is," Jack said, "you're not a cop at all?"

Fuck.

She took a step back, away from them both.

With one hand still securing Jack's wrist, Kyle leaned the shotgun against the wall and pulled a set of handcuffs from his back pocket.

Erica watched, helpless, as Jack threw his shoulder into Kyle's chest, throwing him backward, and then lunged for the weapon. He spun and fired a shot in her direction.

The buckshot hit the door beside her, sending chunks of wood and splinters flying past her head.

She grabbed a fire extinguisher from the wall and threw it as hard as she could. There was a loud metallic *CLUNK* as it slammed into the side of his head.

He dropped the gun as he fell.

She followed the weapon as it slid across the floor, then dove on top of it and rolled to the side, racked the slide, and brought it to bear on Jack.

He was gone.

She pushed herself to her feet.

45

Erica burst through the emergency entrance doors and quickly scanned the parking lot, looking for Jack.

"Melissa!" She turned to see Kyle push through the glass doors. He looked as if he were in pain. He doubled over and held onto his side as she leveled the shotgun at him.

His hands raised high enough that she could see they were empty, and he winced. She noticed the wound on his side.

She lowered the gun. "You're hurt."

"It's a graze. I'll be fine." He pressed his hands back into his side. "A lot of folks are worried about you."

"Worried about *me*?"

"You and John Doe. We need to know what happened at the inn."

The inn?

"That's what this is about? The inn?" She lowered the gun. Over his shoulder, through the large glass windows, she noticed three deputies rushing toward them.

She recalled the conversation she'd overheard earlier, him walking Jack out of the emergency room in handcuffs, and the conversation about Chicago.

If he doesn't know, then the plan could still work.

"Not here. Not now. I'll be in touch."

She leaned down, placed the shotgun on the ground, then turned and ran.

Kyle took a step forward and briefly considered running after her. His side argued against it.

"Kyle!" Serena stopped next to him, closely followed by Bob and Nathan. "You're shot!"

He nodded. "Yes, I know."

She pulled his hand away from his side and lifted the bottom of his shirt.

"I'm alright. It just grazed me."

Bob's head was tilted to the side. He appeared to be taking a mental photo of the wound. "Does it hurt?"

Kyle frowned. "A little, yeah."

"What happened?" Serena asked as Nathan retrieved the weapon from the ground.

"It was Jack," Kyle said. "I had him cornered, but he got away." He took a breath. "Believe it or not, it was Melissa who saved me."

"Melissa?"

He nodded. "You just missed her. She ran that way." He motioned with his chin toward the direction she'd gone.

Serena took a step back and eyed him up and down.

"What?" He asked.

"I'm looking for holes."

"I'm *fine*."

She grabbed his arm, pulled him back inside, then led him to the waiting room where she spun him around and gently pushed him into one of the chairs.

She took a few steps toward the nurse's station, then stopped, turned back, and pointed her index finger at him. "Stay."

He was too tired to argue. He nodded.

"I'm serious."

"I know."

She sighed. Nathan and Bob were standing nearby. She motioned them over. "Keep an eye on him."

46

Kyle gently pulled his shirt over the newly dressed wound and sat on the edge of the bed.

Serena had just left after dropping him off, helping him into the house, and making sure he knew which medication to take and when.

After almost an hour of "yes, ma'am's," he was finally alone.

His gaze fell on the banker's box on the bed beside him: his dad's old case files. He'd found it while cleaning the house after the funeral and brought it home.

He started reading the files four months ago, just before he took over as acting sheriff, and he still hadn't fully come to terms with the information contained inside.

He retrieved a folder, pulled out a stack of photos, and flipped through them.

He paused at one that showed the mayor having lunch with a man at an unfamiliar restaurant. He'd seen this photo many times before.

The next photo showed them shaking hands, and then, in the next, the man was climbing into a dark blue Lincoln Towncar.

The last photo was a closeup of the vehicle's license plate.

He flipped this one over and read the hand-written note scribbled on the back, in his dad's handwriting: *"Tony Lombardi, Chicago."*

He set the photos on the bed to his right and retrieved a piece of paper that was paper clipped to the inside cover of the folder. His dad had written:

March 23, 1990. Chicago.

Hawthorne met with Lombardi again. I couldn't get close enough to hear what they were saying, but whatever it was, Tony didn't like it. He stormed out of the restaurant and got in his car. Armand came out after him, apologizing about something, but Tony wasn't hearing it.

There wasn't anything else in this folder. He collected the photos from the bed, slipped them back into the folder, then placed them all into the box. He pulled out the next one. There was one piece of paper in it.

April 3, 1990.

I've been following them for three months now, and I've finally pieced some things together: 1) Tony Lombardi is a drug king, of sorts, out of Chicago. He gets his shipments from Cuba and sends them to several states for distribution. 2) Armand Hawthorne is one of his distributors. He gets the shipment, breaks it down into smaller packages, then sends it out to the street-level dealers. 3) The shipments seem to be on a regular schedule, and the next one is set to come in next week.

He reached across the bed, grabbed another photo he'd set aside earlier, and read the name on the back of it: *Erica Hawthorne, Armand's daughter, mother unknown.*

He flipped it over and examined the image of Armand Hawthorne hugging a young woman who looked suspiciously like Erica.

"I thought you looked familiar."

47

The light flicked on, and the room illuminated in a soft, yellow glow.

"Hi, Dad."

Armand jumped and turned toward the voice. "Jesus, Erica. Are you trying to give me a heart attack?"

If only.

She was sitting in a brown leather chair in the far corner, swirling a glass of amber liquid.

"What are you doing here?"

She set the glass on the table beside her and stood. "I had to see you. Things are getting out of hand."

"Did Mary see you come in?"

Erica shrugged. "That witch? I don't think she's even here."

Armand grabbed her upper arm and guided her toward the door. "You can't be here. It's too dangerous."

"You're being paranoid."

He stopped and spun her to face him. "Why *are* you here?"

"Can't a girl just pop in to see her daddy?"

He gave her a look of disapproval.

"Fine. I wanted to give you an update. And I need your help with something."

"An update? You could have called for that."

"I could have."

He let go of her arm, crossed to his desk, and lowered himself into his chair. "What is it?"

She plopped into one of the chairs across from him. "Jack. I don't know how much longer I can keep dodging him."

"That's something you need to figure out. I have my own

problems."

"The sheriff's son? How's that going?"

"Not good. He's not like his dad. It's going to take time."

"We don't have time. If he doesn't get Jack off my ass, this will all have been for nothing."

"I know that. This was *my* plan, remember?"

Erica leaned forward. "Yes, I remember. I also remember you saying, 'Don't worry, Erica, everything will be fine. We can do this.' Now I've done my part. You need to do yours."

Armand met her gaze directly. "Have you?"

"What do you mean?"

"Tell me what happened with Keith."

She sat back in the chair and crossed her legs at the ankles. She smoothed the bottom of her tan shirt across her lap. "Back in Chicago, everything was going as planned. He was getting his shipment from Jack, and when they weren't looking, I took the packages from the trunk of Jack's car. It went flawless."

"Did they see you?"

"No. I stayed in the shadows. They didn't even know I was there. Later, after we got back to the apartment, Jack burst in, demanding to know where his stuff was, and he accused Keith of stealing it. Keith denied knowing anything about it, then Jack started punching him and threatening to shoot him." She paused and took a few breaths. "Then Keith pointed at me and said *I* must have taken them. Jack turned toward me, and I ran out of the apartment. I thought I'd lost him, but he found me at the bus station."

"And the bag?"

"I hid it in the lockers, just like you said. It's there now."

"The key?"

"In the treasure box behind Otis's house."

"The one that you and what's his name used to hide stuff in? By the river?"

She nodded. "Floyd. Yes. The box is still there."

Armand watched her reaction when he asked, "And what about Keith?"

"What about him? He crossed me, and I took care of him. He won't be a problem anymore."

"Are you sure? You need to be sure this time."

"Look. The thing that happened at the inn, I had no way of knowing he'd survive being thrown out a second-story window. But it's done now. I found him at the hospital and…"

"The hospital?"

"Yes, the hospital. I smothered him with a pillow. He's not going to be any more trouble."

Armand inhaled audibly and held it. He closed his eyes and pinched the bridge of his nose. "Erica. Tell me you avoided the cameras."

Her head cocked to the side, and her brows furrowed. "Cameras?"

48

Monday, September 24, 1990

Serena slowly stirred her coffee with a thin wooden stick. The diner was quiet. The breakfast crowd had filtered out, and aside from one other person, they had the place to themselves.

"You look nice," Kyle said.

She smiled at him. She was wearing a dark blue shawl over a black, knee-length dress. Her hair was in a tight bun, placed perfectly on the top of her head. A small gold cross was hanging around her neck on a thin gold chain. "Gracias. I'm not sure I like these shoes. I might take them back."

"Too small?"

"Just a bit. They pinch my toes."

"Can you make it through the memorial?"

"Yeah, I think so."

They were comfortable in the silence that followed, each sipping their coffee while waiting for their food.

Serena looked at him over the rim of her cup. "How's your side?"

"It burns. The doctor said it'll hurt for a while. I have to keep an eye on the bandages and change them every night."

"You still taking your medication?"

He nodded. "Yes, I'm still taking my medication."

She sipped the warm drink, then held the cup close to her face with both hands. It smelled faintly of caramel.

The waitress approached the table and set plates in front of them. Serena waited for her to leave before she spoke again. "So, what's going on?"

"What do you mean?"

"I mean, what's going on? I can tell when something's bothering you."

Kyle shrugged. "I can't talk about it. It's… classified."

"Classified? What does that mean?"

"It means I can't talk about it."

"I know what classified means. *What's* classified?"

He shrugged again.

"You're frustrating."

He grinned and popped a French fry into his mouth. "I know. It's one of my most endearing qualities."

"I wouldn't say that." After setting the cup next to her water glass, she lifted the top bun from her burger, removed two rings of raw onion and set them aside, then re-arranged the three pickle slices.

She picked up a napkin and wiped her fingers, then re-folded it and carefully set it back on the table. "It's funny how things work, isn't it? Two days ago, you were in charge. Then everything blew up, and now you're suspended, and *I'm* in charge. I don't like it."

"I don't know. I think it suits you."

She reassembled the sandwich and took a small bite, washed it down with a sip of water, then glanced over her shoulder.

She tapped her finger on the table.

"What?" he asked.

"Nada. Forget it."

He leaned back in the booth and crossed his arms. "Tell me."

49

Serena sighed. She briefly met his eye, then quickly glanced away. She leaned toward him. She noticed that the diner staff were all in the kitchen to her left.

She lowered her voice. "Do you remember when my sister brought you home to meet our parents?"

"Christina? That was what, eighth grade?"

"You were both in ninth. I was in seventh. You were wearing that black leather jacket. Your hair was a mess, spiked up with an entire bottle of gel, and you had that stupid cross hanging from your ear. You looked like that kid from *The Breakfast Club*."

He smiled. "I loved that jacket. I wonder what happened to it."

"I hated it. You looked like an idiot."

"You didn't like me that much back then."

"I didn't. I thought you were a ducha."

"Why's that?"

"I don't know. Maybe because you kept taking my sister away from me? We used to play games all the time, and she'd read to me before bed. She was my best friend. Then she met you, and everything changed. She was never home."

He rubbed his thumb back and forth across his bottom lip. "When did that change?"

She smiled. "I remember the exact night, actually. It was my fourteenth birthday. Do you remember that?"

"That was the night we went to Comic Con."

She nodded. "I cried when Christina told me you were taking her. I wanted to go so bad, but Mom wouldn't let me. She said I had to spend time with the family. Everyone had flown in to see me."

"I remember the look on your face when I came to pick her up. You were standing at the top of the stairs in that pale green and white dress; your hair was done up in curls. And those braces…"

"I hated those braces."

"I thought they were cute."

"Then you talked to my mom and convinced her to let me go. You told her it was my birthday present. When we got to the car, and you took off your jacket, you were wearing that gold *Star Trek* shirt. You were a completely different person."

He smiled. "It would have destroyed my reputation if anyone from school saw me like that."

"And when we got there, you held my hand all night so I wouldn't get lost."

"As I recall, every time I tried to hold hands with Christina, you would insert yourself between us. I assumed it was because you didn't want us together."

She smiled.

"So, why are you bringing this up now?"

She reached across the table and took both his hands in hers. "We've been through a lot, you and I. You're my mejor amigo, my best friend." She paused. "I can tell when something's bothering you. What's going on?"

"I want to tell you. I do. But I can't. Not yet."

"When?"

He shrugged.

"You used to tell me everything."

"I know. I'm sorry, it's just…."

"Classified?" She sighed. "You know, I'm technically your boss now. I can make you tell me."

He took a deep breath, held it briefly, then shrugged. "You can try."

Lauren stepped up to the table and flashed Kyle a huge smile. "Hey, you two. How's everything?"

Serena let his hands go, lifted her coffee cup, and hid her face behind it. She eyed Lauren over the rim. "Peachy."

50

Erica took a sip of sweet tea, flicking her tongue against the semi-sharp edge of the straw. She pulled the plastic red cup away from her mouth and stirred the drink, pushing the ice cubes to the bottom and watched as they floated back to the top, then glanced out the window for the millionth time in the last half hour.

The clock behind the counter read 1:35.

He's late.

A waitress strolled up to the booth and smiled down at her. "Getcha anything else, hun?"

She smiled back. "No, thank you. Just the check."

The waitress nodded and made her way back to the register.

Erica took one last, long pull on the tea, then stood and dropped a twenty-dollar bill on the table. She passed the waitress on her way to the door. "I left it on the table. Keep the change."

"Thank you. Have a good one!"

Have a good one. What does that even mean? Have a good what, exactly?

She leaned against the door and stepped out into the bright sunlight. The air had a chill to it.

Probably from that storm they keep talking about on the radio.

She glanced over at the mountains in the west. Sure enough, the sky was darker now than it had been earlier that morning. She fished a keyring from her pocket and crossed the lot to her car.

Someone grabbed her arm from behind. "Hi there." It was Jack. "Remember me?"

She started to scream, to yell for help, when she felt something press into her ribs.

"Not a word, or I swear to God, I'll end you right here. Where's your car?"

She nodded toward the Concord, and Jack gently pushed her in that direction.

"Unlock it," he said, "and get in."

She slid in behind the wheel as he dropped into the back seat behind her.

"Start the car. Drive."

"To where?"

"I don't give a fuck. Just drive."

Kyle glanced at the clock on the radio in time to see it change from 1:29 to 1:30. It had been just over an hour since he'd left Serena at the diner. He'd told her he needed to run home and grab something really quick; then he'd meet her at the church.

That was before he'd found the note that someone had tucked under the windshield wiper of his Jeep.

Diner, it had said. *County Road 611–Abingdon, 1:30.* He knew the place. As a teenager, he'd spent a lot of time driving around up there, taking his dad's 4-wheel drive pickup for joyrides in the mountains.

He slowed as he approached an intersection. The left turn arrow was red, and he stopped. A red flatbed truck was in front of him.

It seemed like the light took forever to change. When it finally did, the truck slowly moved forward and stopped again as several vehicles drove through the intersection from the other direction.

He glimpsed an old car coming toward him from the left. It looked to be late 70s or early 80s. It was brown, with a few rust spots on the front fender. The chrome front bumper was also rusting in some spots. As the car turned to its right and drove past, he got a good look at the driver.

Erica?

51

Erica glanced up at the rear-view mirror and saw that Jack was looking out the back window.

Normally, she would have enjoyed the scenery. She always felt at home on these mountainside back roads; their quiet farms, thick, lush forests, and spattering of old, abandoned houses.

It was different, however, when there was a man with a gun in the back seat.

Jack was focused on whatever had caught his eye behind them, and she slowly dropped her right hand down to her waist, where she felt the pistol gently digging into her side.

"Both hands on the wheel!"

She did as she was told and firmly grabbed the steering wheel.

"Slow down. Up here, just past the church. Turn right."

She noticed an old white church up ahead on the left. Just past that, a gravel road peeked out from the trees. "How did you find me?"

"Word of advice," he said as he turned to look out the rear window. "If you're hiding from someone, it's not a good idea to leave people notes saying where you're going."

Kyle hung back, matching the car's speed as best he could. He didn't want to get too close. He was certain he had seen someone sitting in the back seat, and he was sure it was Jack. If it was, he didn't want to spook him.

He briefly lost sight of the car as it followed a curve in the road, then saw the taillights as it slowed, then turned right onto a gravel road.

Not wanting to get too close, he pulled into the parking lot of a church and waited. That road led north and followed a stream through the mountains. There were no actual towns up that way, just farms and trees. Whatever Jack was planning, Erica wouldn't be coming out alive.

He pulled out of the lot and turned onto the gravel road. He was far enough back that he couldn't see the car, but he could still see the faint cloud of white dirt it had kicked up.

Occasionally, he would glimpse a house hidden away in the trees, but otherwise, there were no signs of civilization.

He followed the road for about five minutes, easing up on the gas just a little when the dust cloud started thickening.

A yellow sign warned of a sharp curve ahead, and he slowed. The "curve" was, in fact, an almost ninety-degree angle. When the road straightened again, he noticed the dust cloud was gone.

He pulled the Jeep to a stop and glanced at his side mirror, then slid the gear lever into park and climbed out. It was quiet. There were no birds singing, leaves rustling, or engine sounds.

He took a few steps toward the rear of the Jeep and looked back at the way he'd come.

There was a dust cloud before the curve but not after. Where in the hell did they go?

52

"Where's Kyle?" Nathan asked.

Serena glanced around the church, examining everyone's faces. "I don't know. He should be here by now." She raised a tissue and dabbed it under her eye. Three rows up, Leo's family was accepting condolences. His father was shaking Mayor Hawthorne's hand. His mother stood next to him, holding back tears as she looked over the photos of her son that were meticulously placed inside a heart-shaped arrangement of red and white flowers. She removed a Polaroid photo of a very young Leo, wearing a leather cowboy vest, boots, and hat, and clutched it close to her chest before returning to her seat.

She didn't see Leo's brother or sister. She thought for sure that they would have come home for this.

She caught movement out of the corner of her eye and glanced up to see Armand approaching. She quickly looked away and attempted to hide her face behind the tissue.

I hope he didn't see me. Keep walking. Keep walking. Don't stop. Please keep walking.

"Sheriff," he said as he kneeled next to her.

Mierda.

"Have you seen Kyle?"

She avoided his gaze. "No, I haven't."

"Do you know if he's coming?"

"As far as I know. Excuse me." She stood, squeezed past Nathan, and made her way toward the exit, where she pushed open the large wooden door. Sunlight blasted her face, forcing her to squint as she descended the steps, made her way to the payphone on the corner, and dialed Kyle's number.

"Hi, you've reached Kyle Lorne. Leave a message."

She hung up the phone.

"I don't think he's coming."

She turned to see Lauren. "Why do you say that?"

"He was supposed to give me a ride. He said he'd call me before he left to pick me up. He never did. Call, I mean. Every time I try to call him, I get his answering machine."

Serena nodded. "Thank you, Lauren. I'll give him a little longer. Maybe his pain meds are messing with him."

Nathan poked his head out of the door. He held his hand over his eyes as he called out. "Serena, they're starting."

She glanced down at her watch. "Okay, thanks."

Serena stepped out of the church, with Nathan and Bob close behind.

"That was a beautiful service," Bob said.

"Yes, it was. I still can't believe he's gone," Nathan replied.

She was focused. She pulled her sunglasses from her purse and slid them on. "Nathan, head back to the hospital. Talk to security, the administrator, or whoever you need to. Try to get copies of all of the camera footage from yesterday. And talk to Otis; I want to know exactly what Jack said to him. And I want to know where he went when he left the building. Was he still driving our cruiser? Which way did he go? Did he talk to anyone else while he was there?"

Nathan nodded. "Copy, Boss."

"Bob, go back to the station. Contact the surrounding counties and see if they've had any luck with that BOLO on our cruiser. If it pops up anywhere, I want to know immediately."

"Got it."

"What about you?" Nathan asked.

"I'm gonna go find Kyle."

53

Serena parked the Cabriolet on the street in front of Kyle's single-story brick ranch house. His Jeep was nowhere to be seen.

It might be in the garage.

She grabbed her radio and climbed out of the car. Her 2-inch heeled shoes clicked on the sidewalk as she approached the front door. She pressed the doorbell and listened to the chime.

There was no reply. She checked the doorknob.

Locked.

She slipped her feet out of her shoes, stepped off the small porch and into the dirt patch between the house and the bushes, then inched her way toward the large double-paned windows and peered into the living room: nothing looked out of place, and there was no sign of Kyle.

Leaving her shoes behind, she made her way up the driveway to the side of the house, where she stood on her tiptoes to see through the kitchen window. Still nothing. She rounded the house and, as she approached the garage, glanced over her shoulder and noticed that the back door was slightly ajar.

She cautiously crept over to it and listened for any movement inside. She didn't hear anything.

She tugged on the hem of her black dress and pulled a stainless Walther PPK from the holster that was strapped to her thigh, then slowly pushed the door wide enough to pass through.

She stood in the dining room, the tiled floor cooler than the ground outside. The faint smell of stale coffee drifted from the kitchen on her left. Directly in front of her was the living room, and a hallway to her right led to the two bedrooms in the back.

Carefully, she tiptoed through the dining room and peered around the corner. She didn't hear anything, and she didn't see any movement as she slowly made her way toward the first bedroom on her right. The door was wide open, and the room was empty. The next door was the bathroom, also empty, and she noticed that the seat on the toilet was up. She shook her head.

Typical.

The door at the end of the hall was the master bedroom. That door was closed, but she noticed shadows moving through the gap at the bottom.

Rising onto the balls of her feet, she crept up to the door and cautiously pressed her ear against it. She didn't hear anything. She waited for a few seconds. "Kyle, you in there?"

There was no answer. The shadows were still moving.

"If you're in there, I'm coming in."

She reached for the doorknob, slowly twisted it, and opened the door.

The room was empty. Across from her, through the window on the other side, tree limbs were swaying with the breeze.

As she raised the bottom of her dress and holstered the pistol, she noticed a banker's box on the bed, and several folders were laid out next to it.

She picked up the nearest one.

Clipped inside the front cover was a photo of Mayor Hawthorne. She found a note on the back.

"Que demonios? What the hell were you investigating?" She set the folder down and picked up a photo that was off to the side.

"Melissa? Why would Henry have a photo of..." She flipped it over. "Dios Mio. Erica Hawthorne?"

Her radio hissed.

"Boss," it was Nathan.

"Go ahead."

"I found something at the hospital you need to see. Can you meet me here?"

54

"What am I looking at?" Serena stood behind Nathan, who was pushing a computer mouse around on the desk. The hospital's head of security was behind her, leaning against the wall beside the door.

The camera view on the monitor showed the hallway outside one of the recovery rooms, where a security officer sat, reading a newspaper.

"Watch." Nathan clicked the mouse, and the video started playing.

Something seemed to catch the security officer's attention, and he jumped from his chair and ran off-screen to his right. Two seconds later, someone wearing jeans and a gray hoodie rushed past the camera and entered the room.

"Who was that?" She asked.

"I don't know. We can't see his face from this angle."

She turned to the security supervisor. "Are there any other cameras covering this room?"

He shook his head. "I'm afraid not. Just that one."

Nathan clicked a button on the mouse. "Keep watching."

They couldn't see anything moving inside the room except for shadows.

Then the figure ran back out, past the camera, and was gone again.

A few more seconds passed, then, several nurses rushed into the room.

She leaned closer to the monitor. "What's going on?"

"This was when they logged our John Doe's time of death."

She glanced down at the time stamp on the monitor. "Can you play that back? To when that person left the room? Can we see his face?"

"Let's see." He pushed the mouse around and clicked a few more times, then stopped the playback just before the person passed through the door. "I'll go frame-by-frame." He slowly advanced the video until the person's face was visible. He leaned in closer and squinted at the screen, attempting to get a good look. "Who is that?"

"You have got to be shitting me," Serena said.

Nathan glanced up. "Boss?"

She turned and met his eye, and her head cocked to the side. "That's Erica."

"Erica?"

"That's our Jane Doe from Beverly's. Erica Hawthorne."

If Nathan attempted to hide his surprise, he failed. "Hawthorne? As in…"

She nodded. "As in Mayor Hawthorne's daughter."

He pushed himself away from the desk and swiveled his chair to face her. "I have so many questions right now, but I'll stick with the obvious. When the hell did the mayor have a daughter?"

55

She tugged as hard as she could, but the zip ties binding Erica's hands wouldn't budge. "What are we waiting for? I've been sitting here for almost an hour."

Jack stopped pacing and turned toward her. He glanced at his watch.

She scrutinized his every move. "I'm sorry. Do you have a date? I can leave."

He reached down and smacked the back of his hand against her cheek.

"Ow."

"I owed you that."

The sound of a car outside grabbed his attention, and he crossed the room to look through a broken window. He glanced at her over his shoulder, then back to whatever was happening outside.

She was in what appeared to be an Old-West style cantina. She was sitting in an antique wooden chair in the middle of the room. To her left, she saw an old bar, complete with hundred-year-old whiskey bottles lining the wall. Behind her was a dusty piano and, beyond that, a staircase that led to the second floor. The front door was comprised of two small swinging doors.

She'd been here before, years ago, when she and her friends occasionally skipped school.

"Stay here," Jack said as he pushed through the doors.

She tugged again at her restraints. "Really?"

She heard two car doors slam shut, then talking. The voices sounded muffled, and she couldn't understand what they were saying.

Jack returned, followed by a man in a light gray suit.

He said something to Jack in a language that she didn't understand.

Is that Spanish?

Jack nodded, then looked at Erica. "Where's the duffle bag?"

"What duffle bag?"

The man spoke again.

Definitely Spanish.

"The duffel bag that your boyfriend stole from me."

She shrugged. "I have no idea what you're talking about."

He took three steps toward her and raised his hand.

"Stop!" the newcomer yelled.

Jack froze and looked back at the man in the suit.

He said something to Jack. "He said if you don't tell him what he wants to know, he won't stop me next time."

"I can't tell you what I don't know."

Jack glanced back at the man in the suit, who motioned toward the door. Jack turned, crossed the room, then exited the building.

The man grabbed the back of a chair and slowly dragged it toward her. It made an awful sound as it scraped against the old wood floor. He lined it up to face her, brushed off a layer of dirt, then sat down.

"You know who I am?" His English wasn't all that great.

She shook her head.

"Is probably for better. I represent a very powerful man back home in Cuba."

His accent was thick. He pronounced the last word *KOO-Buh*.

"What do you want with me?"

He tilted his head to the side as he eyed her up and down. "You and your boyfriend took something from us. Something very valuable. We want it back."

"Look, I'm sorry, but I don't know…"

"Shhh." He slid his hand into his jacket pocket and pulled out a small folding knife. "I'm going to give you one chance to tell me where you hid that bag and then I'm going to start carving into that pretty little face of yours." He opened the knife, moved in close, and pressed it against her cheek under her left eye.

She felt her skin give way as the razor-sharp blade drew blood. "Listen, if those drugs are that important to you, I'll go get them right now."

He smiled. "No, no. It's not the drugs we want. We want what's *inside* them."

"I don't understand. What's inside them?"

He pressed a little harder with the blade. Her skin felt as if it were on fire. "Where is the bag?"

I'm going to kill you.

"Chicago."

He stood and smiled at her. "Good." He turned and started for the door. "Mister Jenkins!"

Jack popped his head through the top of the doors.

"Twenty-four hours. We'll be in touch with further instructions."

56

Jack stood over Erica, examining the cut on her face. "Looks like it hurts."

"I've had worse."

He nodded. "So, where's the bag?"

"Who was that psycho?"

"That psycho is a very dangerous man. And he works for an even more dangerous man. One that you do *not* want to piss off."

She stared up at him. "He called you Mister Jenkins."

"Don't worry about that. What did you tell him?"

She inhaled. "The truth. I told him that the bag is in a locker in Chicago. At the bus station."

"Chicago? How are we supposed to..." he dropped into the empty chair across from her. "Fuck." His head fell forward, and he pressed the palms of his hands into his eyes. "That's not enough time." He looked back up at her. "We're both dead." He stood and started pacing. Finally, he stopped and faced her. "I might as well just kill us both right now. That's how fucked we are." His eyes narrowed, and his head cocked to the side. "Actually, there might be another option."

"There is?"

"He wants the key to his storage unit. We can get that without going anywhere."

"Storage unit? What storage unit?"

He was quiet for a few seconds as if contemplating something. "Your dad and me, we have a side business going that we've kept from everyone. We sold some product to the Cubans, and inside that bag is the key to the drop-off point - the storage unit."

"Product? You mean drugs."

"Not exactly. The point is your dad has a spare key in his office."

"There you go. All we need to do is go ask him for it."

"It's not that simple. He doesn't know about this fuck up. He's not gonna be happy about it, that's for damn sure. He's got a good relationship with the Cubans, and the last thing he wants to do is to screw it up." He looked into her eyes. "I'm going to need your help to get it. Like it or not, missy, you and me, we're in this together now."

I don't see as if I have a choice.

"So, what's the plan?"

57

Tuesday, September 25, 1990

Serena felt the chill from the morning air as she examined the sizeable wooden door before her. She glanced to her right, at the fog that was rolling in across the front yard, then turned back to the intricate woodwork with its sandblasted glass panels. It looked heavy. She knocked. It felt heavy. She counted thirty seconds before she heard the deadbolt click from the other side. When the door opened, Mary Hawthorne stood there, smiling at her.

"Serena." She seemed surprised to see her.

"Good morning, Mary."

"Good morning. Please, come in."

She wiped her feet on the bristly WELCOME mat before stepping inside the large foyer. To her right was the dining room, where she saw a large wooden table adorned with flowers and expensive-looking China.

Directly in front of her was a winding staircase that opened into a large area on the second floor.

"I assume you're here to see Armand."

"I am. Is he here?"

"Yes, he is. This way."

She led Serena through the large living room, where the smell of a recent fire lingered in the air. She noticed that the fireplace's metal grate was pulled to one side, and a metal poker was leaning against it.

Mary gently knocked on another door, then tugged it to the side. She motioned for Serena to enter.

Armand was sitting behind his desk. "Sheriff. What brings you out this early?"

She slowly approached the desk. The flowers outside the massive window behind him distracted her.

He must have seen the look on her face. "Beautiful, isn't it?" He rose from his chair.

She nodded. She was in awe of the vibrant colors as the rising sun shone on them.

"Mary takes great pride in those."

"I can tell."

He hesitated for a moment. "What can I do for you, Sheriff?"

You can go to hell, for starters.

She pulled a printout of a still frame from a security camera from her pocket and held it up for him to see. "I'm looking for your daughter, Mayor. Have you seen her?"

He rushed to the door and quickly shut it. "What's the hell's the matter with you? Have you no decency?"

"It's a simple question."

His eyes fell on the young woman in the photo. "What makes you think she's my daughter?"

"I don't have time for games. Where is she?"

He took the photo from her. "What do you want with... this woman?"

"She's a person of interest. I need to ask her some questions."

"Questions? Like what?"

"You know I can't discuss an ongoing investigation."

"Sheriff, I'm privy to everything that goes on in this town. I'll find out whether you tell me or not."

She inhaled, then stopped herself before she spoke. She could feel the handcuffs on her duty belt calling to her. It took all of her willpower not to pull them out and slap them on his wrists.

"You think she had something to do with the death of that young man at the hospital?"

And how do you know about that?

"I didn't say that. I just want to know what she was doing there."

His head cocked to the side.

He turned and re-opened the door. "I'm sorry, Sheriff, I can't help you."

You can.

"You do know, sir, that impeding an investigation is a crime."

His face turned red. "I don't need you to cite the laws to me, Sheriff. Don't for a second forget who you're talking to."

She nodded.

If this is how you want to play it…

She retrieved the photo from him, folded it, and slipped it back into her pocket. "Thank you for your time, Mayor. I'll see myself out." She found her way to the front door, grabbed the knob, and pulled it open.

Jack was standing there, mere inches away, his fist frozen in the air as if he were in mid-swing of knocking.

Her eyes grew wide, and her right arm instinctively lashed out. The heel of her hand slammed into his face. She heard a crack, and he stumbled back a few steps, then grabbed his face with both hands.

"Agh! You broke my fucking nose!" His voice was nasally and wet.

She saw blood seeping from between his fingers.

"I'm gonna kill you, Mexican Puta!" One of his hands dropped toward what looked like the handle of a pistol.

She took a step forward, pivoted on her left leg, and kicked out to the side with her right foot. His head jerked backward as her heel contacted his chin, and he fell to the ground, his arms splayed to his sides.

"I'm Colombian, asshole." She pulled the handcuffs from her belt and kneeled next to him.

58

Erica smiled as she watched the lady cop…

Serena?

… put Jack in the back seat of the police car and close the door. He appeared dazed from being kicked in the face.

I like this plan so far.

She waited until they were gone before she left the safety of the bushes and started for the house. She had just left her hiding spot when the front door opened, and Armand stepped out. He glanced down at the lawn where Jack had been laying, shook his head, then crossed over to the Maserati and climbed in.

After the car turned onto the street and was out of sight, she sprinted to the front door.

Please be open. Please be open.

It was unlocked.

Thank you!

She entered the house and went straight to his office.

After sliding the door closed behind her, she lowered herself into her father's chair, feeling the soft leather encompass her like a giant hug. She swiveled left and right as she surveyed the office, watching the shadows cast from the window as they played over the books.

"If I were a secret key, where would I be hiding?"

She tugged on the drawers of the desk. They were all locked except for one, and the only thing it contained was an empty manila folder. It had folds and creases, as if it once held something lumpy.

She admired the leather-bound first editions and law references and noticed one book that looked out of place. The spine was brown, designed to look like leather, but it was shiny, printed instead of wrapped. She stood and crossed the room. As she got closer, she could make out the words written on it. "From the Library of Safety Storage, Inc."

Too easy.

She ran her finger down the spine.

Definitely not leather.

Hooking her index finger over the top edge, she pulled it from the bookcase.

It was light for its size.

She flipped the cover open and discovered that it was hollow. A key and a small, folded piece of paper were taped inside.

She pulled the paper free and unfolded it. An address in Sutherland, North Carolina, was written in capital block letters.

She heard a door close somewhere in the house and shoved the slip of paper and the key into her pocket, then put the book back on the shelf where she found it.

That must be Dad's wife. Time to go.

59

Jack was staring at her through the rearview mirror. Serena reached up and pushed it to the side so she didn't have to look at his face.

"Don't be like that."

She glanced over her shoulder. "How are those handcuffs? Too tight?"

"Yeah, a bit. My hands are going numb."

"Good. Now shut up before I come back there and tighten them some more."

He grinned at her. "Careful, Deputy. That's borderline brutality."

"It's Sheriff."

"My apologies, Sheriff. Seriously, you think you can loosen these things a little?"

"Sure. As soon as we get back to the station, I'll have Leo do that."

He snorted and looked out the window. "You're not still sore about that, are you? Look, it wasn't personal. He was in the way of my mission, and things got out of hand."

"Out of hand? You snapped his neck!"

"Yeah, but I did apologize to him after."

She shot him another look over her shoulder. "You're sick. And you're gonna spend the rest of your miserable life behind bars."

"Oh, I wouldn't be too sure about that."

She turned her focus to the road. The next few miles were quiet. It was Jack who finally broke the silence. "Hey, Sheriff. I'm not feeling so well. Are we almost there?"

She readjusted the mirror. It looked like he was having a difficult time breathing. His head bobbed to the side, and his eyelids were half closed. Blood was trickling from his broken nose. "You okay back there?"

His head dropped forward, and a split second later, he fell onto his side.

"Mierda." She slowed the car, pulled over to the side of the road, and grabbed the microphone from the clip on the radio. "Parker, this is Rios."

A few seconds passed. "Hey, Sheriff. You almost here?"

"I'm still fifteen minutes out. Something's wrong with my prisoner. Can you get an ambulance started my way? I'm half a mile north of the boat ramp at Lake Sturgeon."

"On it. You need me out there?"

"Stand by. I'll let you know in a sec." She threw the gear shifter into park, pushed the door open with her shoulder, then jumped out of the car and reached for the handle on the back door.

She was caught off guard when the door flung open, and Jack's feet lashed out. The force from the kick threw her onto her back. She scooted away from him and pushed herself up.

"This has been fun, sheriff, but it's time I get going. Thanks for the ride, though."

He dangled the handcuffs over her before letting them drop. They bounced off her leg and fell onto the street.

"How did you...?"

He winked at her. "That's my little secret. Now, if you don't mind, I'll be borrowing your car for a while."

She grabbed the handle of her pistol; her thumb popped open the safety strap of the holster.

Jack shook his head. "Now, I wouldn't be doing that unless you want to end up like Deputy Leo."

She pulled her hand away.

"Good choice." He took a step closer. "There's just one more thing."

The last thing she saw before she lost consciousness was the bottom of his shoe rushing at her face.

60

Carolyn adjusted the glasses on her nose. She waited as Kyle made himself comfortable in the chair.

"How have you been since the last time we talked?"

"Not that great, really. I'm in a tough spot right now."

"How so?"

"I'm sure you've heard by now that Leo is gone."

"I did hear that. I'm sorry. I know you were close."

He nodded. "And I lost my job."

"You lost your job? How did that happen?"

"Not really lost it. I was suspended. The mayor didn't like my performance."

"Is he able to do that?"

"Until we get a permanent sheriff, he's basically in charge. Something in the town charter left over from last century."

"Oh."

He instinctively felt for the loose string, then remembered it wasn't there anymore. Instead, he found a tiny hole beneath which the cotton filling was poking through.

"So, what have you been doing if you're not working?"

"I got into a fight at the hospital. Oh, and I got shot."

Her eyes grew wide. "You got shot?"

"Not serious. The buckshot grazed my side. Hurts like hell, though."

"I bet it does."

She wrote something in her notebook and readjusted her glasses. "I can tell something's weighing heavily on your mind. Do you want to talk about it?"

"Yes."

"What is it?"

He took a breath. His eyes burned a little as a tear slowly rolled down his cheek.

Carolyn crossed one leg over the other. "Kyle?"

"Something's going to happen, and I can't stop it."

"Something like what?"

He gently pushed the tip of his little finger into the hole, pushing the cotton back into its place. "I can't say. It has to do with work."

"I thought you said you were suspended."

"I am." His finger was lodged in the hole. He gently tugged it, not allowing it to fully pull free. "But I'm not. It's complicated."

"How so?"

He tugged harder, and his finger popped out. He noticed the hole was now a little bigger than it had been a minute ago. "Some decisions were made, and things are in motion that are going to affect a lot of people."

"Including you?"

He weakly smiled. "Especially me."

"How so?"

I wish I could tell you.

"Do you remember when I told you that my dad said I wasn't ready for the job?"

She nodded.

"I know what he really meant. And he was right. I'm *not* ready. But I have the opportunity to pick up where he left off." The tear was nearing the edge of his mouth, and he reached up and wiped it away. He took another deep breath and shrugged. "I just feel like I'm not in control of my life anymore."

"What do you mean?"

"I mean, these decisions, these choices, this path I'm on will lead to somewhere I won't be able to return from. Everything I know, everything I am, will all be gone. Nothing will be the same."

She placed her pencil on the arm of her chair and leaned forward. Her eyebrows furrowed. "That's all very cryptic."

"I know. I wish I could say more, but the less you know, the less anyone knows... I've said too much already."

"But you haven't really said anything."

He stood and reached out his hand. "Thank you, Doctor Young."

She rose from the chair. "Kyle?"

"Thank you for everything."

61

Serena watched from the back of the ambulance as Parker pulled up beside her. He checked the area as he exited the car and headed toward her. She knew what he was looking for. "He took my car."

He shook his head. "He has a propensity of doing that, doesn't he?"

She nodded. "Yours is the last one. You better keep a close eye on it."

He grinned. "How's your head?"

She reached up and touched the bandage on her forehead. "I'll live. He kicked me in the face. I must have lost consciousness because I don't remember anything after that."

"At least he left your gun."

She felt the handle rub against the inside of her arm. "Yeah. There's that."

"So, what now?"

She sighed, then shrugged. "Honestly, I don't know. I can tell you one thing, though, once all of this is over, I'm going to submit a requisition to have GPS installed on all our vehicles."

He chuckled. "Good idea."

He held out his hand and helped her down from the back of the ambulance.

Her radio crackled. "Sheriff, it's Betty."

She unclipped it from her belt. "Go ahead, Betty."

"Sheriff, I've got Doctor Young here. She says she needs to speak with you. She says it's urgent."

"Doctor Young?" Parker said.

"Put her on."

"I just press here?" Doctor Young said.

"Yes, that's it. Just like that. You're transmitting now," Betty answered.

"Oh, she can hear me?"

"Yes, she can hear you."

"Hello? Sheriff?"

"You need to let go of the button when you're done talking."

"Oh, okay, like thi…"

Serena chuckled. "Doctor Young. What can I do for you?"

"Hello, Sheriff, this is Doctor Young."

"Yes, ma'am. How can I help you?"

"I usually don't do this, with client confidentially and all. I just had a conversation that I think you need to know about."

"Okay. What's going on?"

"I don't know if you're aware, but Kyle is a patient of mine."

"He had mentioned it a few times."

"Well, he just left here. The way he was talking… he was definitely worried about something. He wouldn't say what, but I think he's in some sort of trouble."

You have no idea.

"We do have a lot going on right now. He's been under a lot of stress lately."

"I know. He told me. But this seemed… different. He was really worried about something. Something he didn't want to discuss." She hesitated. "There's no easy way to say this, so I'll just say it. He said things that caused me to be concerned."

"He did? Like what?"

"He was saying things about decisions that will affect a lot of people, especially himself, and something that's going to happen that he won't be able to return from. I asked him what he meant, but he wouldn't elaborate any more than that. Then he just left. He thanked me for everything and walked out. I'm worried about him. And I know you two are close, and I thought you should know."

Dios mio, Kyle. What are you up to?

"Did he say where he was going?"

"No. And he didn't confirm our next meeting, so I'm not certain that he's planning on coming back."

"Thank you, Doctor Young. I'll check in on him and make sure he's okay."

"Thank you, sheriff. Please let me know if I can help."

"I will. Bye, Sheriff."

She smiled. "Goodbye, Doctor."

"What's going on with Kyle?" Parker asked.

"I've no idea. Come on. Let's get out of here."

62

Serena observed how the trees farther away rushed past slower than the ones closer to the car. She knew how science worked, of course, but she still believed in the 'magic' of it all.

Suddenly, the forest abruptly gave way to large, open fields, and beyond those, the mountains appeared to be fading as thick fog rolled in from the other side.

Bob slowed the car as they approached an intersection. He turned left, back toward the town.

She was lost in her thoughts, reliving the events from earlier that day when Jack attacked her and stole her car. Interspersed with those thoughts was the brief conversation she'd had with Doctor Young and recalling previous conversations with Kyle, and everything else that had happened this past week.

This is the second time in as many days that he's gone off the grid without so much as a word as to where he's going or what he's doing. I wish he'd let me in.

The car's radio hissed, then Kyle's voice came over the speaker. "Sheriff Rios, you there?"

She grabbed the mic and pressed her thumb into the button. "Kyle! Where are you? Are you okay? I've been trying to reach you."

The radio was silent for a few seconds. "I'm fine. I found my old radio in the bottom of the bag that I keep in my Jeep. I'm headed out of town and I keep losing signal. I wanted to let you know that I'm on my way to the airport in Louisville. I'll be gone for a few days."

"The airport?"

"Yeah. I have something I need to take care of. I'm headed to Chicago."

"Chicago? What's in Chicago?"

"I'll fill you in when I get back. I just want to make sure you're okay. We didn't get to finish our conversation yesterday, and something came up. I missed Leo's memorial."

"You did. We were all worried. I looked for you at your house, but you weren't there."

Bob leaned toward her and whispered, "Tell him about Jack."

She shook her head and mouthed, 'No.'

"Was that Bob?" Kyle asked.

"When will you be back?"

"Two days."

"Call me when you get to Chicago. We need to talk."

"Will do."

The transmission ended with a burst of static.

"He's out of range," she said.

"You should have told him about Jack."

She turned back to the window. They were passing an offshoot of South Holston Lake, and she saw a single boat floating near the water's edge on the far side. Two men had fishing poles in the water. "Yeah. Probably."

63

The car stopped at the gate, and Erica stared at the building on the other side.

Is this the right place?

She lifted the paper from the seat beside her and double-checked the address.

This is it.

She grabbed the crank, lowered the window, and stared at the keypad beside her.

Okay, now what's the secret code?

She typed in the numbers of her dad's birthday. A little red light blinked in the top left corner of the box.

That's not it.

She tried her birthday. The light blinked again.

Dammit.

She glimpsed her reflection in the black glass protecting the security camera seated to the left of the keypad, and for an instant, she saw her mother's face looking back at her.

Wait a minute.

She typed in her mom's birthday.

A green light flashed in the top right corner, and a beep-beep-beep emitted from a speaker box just above it as the gate slid open.

"Seriously, dad?"

She slowly cruised the lot of the self-storage units until she found the one that matched the number stamped on the key. She slid the gear shifter into park, shut off the engine, and climbed out.

The key slid into the padlock easily. As she twisted, the lock popped open.

Inside, the storage unit was dark and dusty, except for a single rug in the middle of the floor. It was maroon and dark blue, with gold trim and frilly edges.

She cautiously approached the rug, examining it as she got closer. But, again, she could see nothing out of the ordinary.

It's just a rug.

She stomped her foot on it. The floor was solid underneath.

Okay, this is weird.

She returned to the entrance and reached for the thick string to pull the door down.

She heard a noise.

What was that?

She stood still, her hand on the string, listening.

There it is again.

It was coming from inside somewhere. It sounded like nails scratching against concrete.

She let go of the string, kneeled next to the rug, and grabbed a corner. It was heavier than it looked, but she managed to move it out of the way.

She saw a very thin seam forming a large square in the floor. On one side was a recessed metal handle, and on the opposite side were two heavy-duty hinges. She slid her fingers through the U-shaped handle and tested the weight.

I can do this. I just need to...

She straightened her back and pulled the handle with both hands. Her leg muscles strained as she stood, but she managed to pull the trapdoor open. The four-inch-thick concrete slab fell to the side, hitting the floor with a loud bang.

She peered into the dark hole that was now in front of her. She couldn't see clearly, but she thought something was moving around down there.

A hand reached up and grabbed her ankle. Startled, she jumped back. "What the fuck?"

Erica stared into the eyes of a young girl, her face dirty, her clothes filthy and torn. "Por favor. Ayudenos. Por favor."

As her eyes adjusted to the dark, she saw that the girl wasn't alone. There were several other children with her, boys and girls, all appearing to be between nine and thirteen years of age. Some of them were crying.

Several of the others quietly spoke up. "Please," one said.

"Let me go," said another.

"I want my mommy."

"We're hungry."

She stared at the faces looking up at her and smiled. "You're making this all too easy for me, Dad."

64

Wednesday, September 26, 1990

"Hi, Serena. It's Deputy Anderson from the Washington County Sheriff's Department. We met last year at that joint training in Bristol."

Serena sandwiched the phone receiver between her shoulder and ear. "Yeah, hi. It's Jason, right?"

"That's right. I wasn't sure if you'd remember."

"How can I forget? How's the baby? What is she, two now?"

"Almost. She'll be two next month."

"She's adorable. Thank you again for showing me those pictures."

"Thanks. She's a handful, that's for sure. So, listen. I'm afraid that this isn't a social call. One of our locals reported an abandoned car behind a restaurant out on 611, just off Rich Valley Road. I responded and found one of your patrol cars. It was just sitting there."

She grabbed a pen and jotted down the information on a legal pad. "611? Behind a restaurant? Can I get that address?" She wrote it down as he gave it to her. "How did it look? Any visible damage?"

"None that I saw. You mentioned in your BOLO that the person who took it was armed and dangerous. Should we be worried up here?"

"It wouldn't hurt to have everyone on alert, just in case. Do you have the resources to have someone sit on it until I can get there? If I leave in the next five minutes, I should be there by…" she flipped her wrist up and glanced at her watch. "Nine, nine-thirty."

"Yeah, I can do that. All of our deputies are out looking for a little girl who went missing from a dance studio this morning, but I can break away and head over there myself and wait for you."

"That seems to be happening a lot lately."

"Yeah, unfortunately, it does."

"I hope you find her."

"Thanks. You and me both."

"I'll fax over a photo of the man we're looking for."

"Sounds good. See you soon."

She hung up the phone. "Bob."

Deputy Parker looked up from the report he was writing. "Yeah, Boss?"

"I'm heading up to Abingdon. They found Leo's car."

"That's great news. Do you want me to come with you?"

She shook her head. "No, thanks. I'll be okay. Someone from the local PD is gonna meet me there."

Bob nodded. "Copy that. I'll call if anything comes up."

She rose from behind her desk and grabbed her jacket and ball cap off the hook on her way out the door.

65

The drive was uneventful. It took Serena exactly one hour and twelve minutes, plenty of time to get lost in her thoughts.

She was worried about Kyle; where was he, what was he doing, is he okay?

It's not like him to just up and disappear like that. No phone call or anything. I wish I knew where he was. If he's alright.

She was worried about when Jack would reappear and what he might do when he did.

If he was brazen enough to attack a law enforcement officer in his own station, what else is he capable of?

And she was worried about what she might find in that car when she got there.

As she pulled to a stop in the front parking lot of the diner, she saw yellow caution tape blocking off the rear lot, with large, bold letters announcing POLICE LINE, DO NOT CROSS sprawled across it. She shut off the car and climbed out. As she approached the tape, Jason emerged from his patrol car, parked a few feet away.

"Jason."

"Serena."

"Thank you for calling."

"Of course." He lifted the tape, and she ducked under it. "I left it just as I found it. Didn't see anything in the seats. No weapons or anything. Was there a shotgun in that harness?"

"Yeah. Judging by your question, can I assume it's gone?"

He nodded. "I'm afraid so."

She scrutinized the car as she slowly approached. There didn't seem to be any damage on the outside.

147

That's a good sign.

She pulled the handle on the driver's door and pulled it open. As Jason had said, the shotgun was missing. She found the keys in the ignition.

Jason was watching through the windshield as she pulled them out. "Who's dumb enough to leave the keys in a car like that?"

"You'd be surprised." She went to the rear of the car, slid one of the keys into the lock, and the trunk sprung open. She saw a shovel, a small length of brown rope, a roll of duct tape, and what looked like a motel key on a yellow triangular keychain. The number 106 was stamped on it.

"You recognize it?"

She picked it up and flipped it over. There were no other identifying marks on it. "No. No, I don't. You?" She held it out for him, and he took it.

He shook his head. "No, sorry." He handed it back.

66

Kyle set his suitcase on the floor and smiled at the young woman behind the desk. "Good afternoon."

She smiled back. "Good afternoon, sir. Are you checking in?"

"I hope so. But I don't have a reservation."

Her smile widened. "That's not a problem. We're typically not very busy during the week." Something behind him caught her attention, and she looked over his shoulder. Her smile faded. "You're back. Joy."

Erica leaned on the counter beside him and slapped four one-hundred-dollar bills onto it. "Nice to see you again, too, Beth." She scanned the lobby. "Two rooms. Adjoining."

Kyle turned toward her. "Melissa?"

"Melissa?" Beth echoed.

"Cut the crap, Kyle. I know you know who I am."

This caught him off guard.

Beth looked at them disapprovingly as she typed on the keyboard. "You're together, then. Smoking or non?"

"Not exactly," Kyle answered. "Non-smoking." He turned back to Erica. "What are you doing here?"

"I followed you." She grabbed a mint from a small bowl on the counter and popped it into her mouth. She smiled at Beth. "Ground floor if you have them."

Beth frowned and continued typing. "Of course."

"You followed me?"

"No, of course not. Don't be silly. I always stay here. It's the only hotel in town that doesn't suck."

"Thanks," Beth rolled her eyes. "That's our motto, actually. 'Stay here, we don't suck.'"

"Look, Beth, as much as I enjoy our little conversations, I just got off a very small plane where I sat next to an old man who was apparently allergic to soap, and I'm kinda tired. Can we get our keys, please?"

Beth frowned again and held out two keys. Erica took them. "112 and 114. Just down the hall, past the elevator on the left. Check-out is 10:30. There's a continental breakfast starting at 6:00 a.m.."

"Yeah," Erica said, "Thanks." She grabbed a small black duffel bag from the floor and crossed the room toward the elevators.

Kyle smiled at Beth again, then picked up his suitcase and followed Erica down the hall. He caught up with her as she unlocked the door and pushed it open. She offered him the key to his room.

"You're next door."

She entered the room, and the door closed, leaving him staring at a tiny peephole.

"Okay then." He let himself into the next room over, set his bag on the bed, and reached for the door separating the two rooms. She was standing in the doorway.

She stepped past him.

"Sure, come on in."

67

He watched as Erica turned and sat on the edge of his bed, gave the room a once-over, and then met his gaze. "My room is nicer."

He stared at her.

She stared back.

He folded his arms and leaned against the open-door frame. "The last time I saw you, you were being held at gunpoint. What happened?"

"He let me go."

"He let you go? After everything I've seen this past week, I find that hard to believe."

"Turns out he and I have a common goal."

"Which is?"

"Staying alive." She leaned back onto the bed.

He uncrossed his arms, went to the desk on the other side of the room, and lowered himself into the fake leather chair.

She sat up and crossed her legs at the ankles. "I saved your life. At the hospital. You owe me."

"Do I?"

"You do." She picked at her fingernails. Her eyebrows furrowed.

He sat silently, watching her.

"I've come across something that I don't know how to handle." She looked at him. "I need help." She leaned back a little, reached into the front pocket of her jeans, and retrieved a key. "Jack and my dad," she watched his face, "your mayor, are working for a drug dealer here in Chicago."

He nodded. "I know."

"Of course you do." She twirled the key in her fingers. "I won't say how, but I came into possession of a duffel bag that was in transit to Millhaven. Dad had me put it in a locker at a bus station here in Chicago and hide the key." She looked away from him and appeared to focus on something on the wall. "After Jack kidnapped me the other day, he took me to that old movie set up in the mountains. He tied me to a chair, and then some angry guy showed up. Jack said he was Cuban. He put a knife to my face." She touched a small cut under her eye. "He said there was a key hidden inside the bag, and he wanted it back. He gave me and Jack twenty-four hours to get it. After he left, Jack said my dad kept a duplicate key in his office, and all we had to do was break in and steal it."

He nodded at the key in her hand. "Is that it?"

"Yes. I found an address, too. In North Carolina." She took another deep breath. "I went there last night to have a look. See what the fuss was all about."

"What did you find?"

She turned toward him and said, "There was a cellar underneath a storage locker. It was… there were…" She took a breath. "It was filled with kids."

This took him by surprise. "Kids?"

She nodded. "It was dark, but if I had to guess, there were maybe fifteen, twenty. The oldest couldn't have been more than twelve or thirteen."

"What did you do?"

"I left them there. I was scared. I was scared of what that Cuban would do to me. Of what Jack would do to me. I didn't sign up for this. I don't know what to do." She held out the key. "I don't want this."

He took it from her. "Do you remember the address?"

She pulled a small, folded piece of paper from her pocket and handed it to him.

He stood. "Thank you for telling me this. I need to make a phone call. I'll be right back."

68

Serena was sitting at her desk, staring at the key with the yellow triangle keychain. Aside from a few deep scratches from years of use, she saw nothing that would tell her where it was from.

She tapped the tip of her pen on the yellow legal pad on her desk and stroked the sore spot on her forehead where Jack had kicked her. Nathan was at the water cooler, refilling his 'World's Best Dad' mug. Betty was sitting at her desk, furiously typing on her keyboard, and Nathan was somewhere in the back of the station, doing... whatever it was he was doing.

Her eyes fell on the glass door of the main office in the far corner. She was used to seeing Kyle sitting there. That had been his room ever since his dad had passed away. It didn't seem right for her to take it over.

"Um. Hey, Boss?"

She looked back at Nathan. His voice was deep, and his thick mustache wiggled as he talked. He'd always reminded her of an actor.

What was his name? Sam Elliott?

He was now giving his full attention to whatever was going on outside the window. He pulled the blinds aside for a better look. "You're not going to believe this."

She rose from her chair and crossed the room to have a look. "What the heck?" She opened the door and stared in disbelief as her missing patrol car pulled into the parking lot with Arnie Willis behind the wheel.

She stepped outside and watched as Arnie attempted to park the car beside her VW. He gave up and left it half in, half out of the spot, shut off the engine, and climbed out.

"Arnie?"

"Hi, Sh-sh-sheriff. I f-f-found your car."

"I see that. I don't know whether to be mad or give you a hug."

His eyes grew wide. "Hug. Definitely."

She walked around the car, examining every inch. She didn't see any new dents, dings, or scratches. Aside from a bit of dirt, it looked exactly as it did the last time she saw it when Jack… "Where did you find it?"

"It was on the d-d-dirt road by the school. It was j-j-just sitting there."

She heard a knock from the rear of the car. "What's that?"

Arnie grinned. "Th-th-that's Wes."

"Come again?" She reached into the car and pulled the keys from the ignition.

"He w-w-wanted to k-k-keep the car. I told him, no, we need to g-g-give it back. He said no. So, I t-t-tricked him and l-l-locked him in the trunk."

She slid the key into the lock. The trunk flew open, and Wes bounded out. He saw his brother near the front of the car and lunged toward him.

Serena scooped him up with both arms and lifted him from the ground. "Easy, Wes."

Wes was angry. She could see it on his face.

"I'm gonna kill you, little twerp!"

She lowered him to the ground and held him against the side of the car. "Easy!"

His eyes met hers, and he held his hands up in the universal 'I surrender' gesture. "Okay. Okay." He eyed Arnie. "You're lucky your girlfriend's here to protect you."

Arnie's face turned red. "She's not my girlfriend!"

"She is too! You want to kiss her!"

"Shut up!"

Wes pursed his lips and made kissing gestures. "Muh muh muh!"

Arnie moved toward him. "I said shut up!"

Serena held her hand up in his direction, halting him from coming any closer. She turned back to Wes. "Cool it. Now."

Wes apparently saw something in her face that instantly changed his attitude. "Okay."

"You good now?"

He nodded. "I'm good."

She pulled away and noticed they had an audience: Bob and Nathan were crossing the lot toward them.

Wes lunged toward Arnie and tackled him to the ground. Wes had his hands around his brother's neck before Serena could react.

Nathan grabbed Wes and pulled him away, while Bob found a handful of Arnie's shirt and dragged him toward the station.

"Enough!" She pointed to Arnie. "Take him inside."

Bob nodded, then guided Arnie toward the front door.

She turned back to Wes. "You. Are we good?"

He nodded.

"I want to hear it. Are we good?"

"We're good."

"Good. Now, go inside, find a chair, and park it. I'm gonna call your mom and have her come pick you up."

His head dropped. "Yes, ma'am."

She turned to Nathan. He was grinning at her. "Don't."

His grin morphed into a full-blown smile. "I didn't say anything."

69

Serena sat in the chair beside Arnie and handed him a plastic cup filled with water.

"Th-th-thank you." He took a small sip of the cool drink.

She nodded. "You're welcome." She glanced across the room at Bob, who was keeping Wes busy. She turned back to Arnie. "You said you found the car behind the school?"

He nodded.

"What were you doing back there?"

"Wes p-p-pulled me out of class. He told the teacher that m-m-mom was in the hospital, and we had to go see her."

"Is she?"

"N-n-no. He just said that to get us out of school."

She frowned.

I need to have a little talk with Wes when this is all over.

"W-w-we took the shortcut home, through the forest. When we got to the dirt road, we saw it sitting there. We thought it was f-f-fate since we b-b-broke that other one. So, we took it. Only..." His head dropped, and he stared at his shoes.

"Only what?"

"Only those guys were there."

"What guys?"

"Th-th-there was a black guy. Big. Lots of muscles, l-l-like a bodybuilder. And a light brown-skinned man, but not black. He spoke with a funny accent. We c-c-couldn't understand anything he said."

"What happened next?"

"They both got into another car. Then they left. W-W-Wes and me, we got in the p-p-police car and left as quick as we could."

"Did you see the other car? The one they got into?"

He nodded.

"What color was it?"

"D-d-dark blue."

"Did it have two doors or four?"

"Four. It was a n-n-1988 Jaguar XJ6. 195 horsepower, aluminum block, zero to sixty in eight seconds flat. T-T-Top speed 136 miles per hour."

"Wow. You really know your cars, don't you?"

He nodded. "I like cars. And I remember things."

"Do you happen to remember seeing the license plate?"

He nodded again. "It was from F-F-Florida. I R L 3 4 F."

"Arnold Willis, you're amazing."

His face turned a deep shade of red, and he beamed with the biggest smile she'd ever seen on him.

She pulled a notepad and pen from her shirt pocket, jotted down the license number, then stood. "Nathan."

"Yeah, Boss?"

She ripped the paper from the notepad and held it out for him. "See if you can track down this license plate. I need to know who it belongs to."

He took it from her. "Will do. You want me to call the boys' mom?"

Across the room, Bob was having a quiet conversation with Wes. She glanced back at Arnie. "Nah, I'll take care of that."

Nathan nodded and returned to his desk. He pulled out his chair, lowered himself into it, and grabbed the phone.

"Did I do good?"

She smiled at him. "You did great."

"Thank you." He gulped down the rest of his water. "C-c-can I get some more?"

"Of course." She reached for the cup, but he pulled it away from her.

"I can get it." He stood and headed toward the water cooler. As he passed her desk, he stopped and turned back to face her.

"Are you staying at that place by the c-c-caverns? We stayed there. After m-m-mom left my dad. They have a pool."

Serena's eyes narrowed. "I'm sorry. What?"

Arnie lifted the yellow keychain from her desk and held it up. "This is from Briscoe's M-m-motor Inn. In Bristol, right?"

70

Thursday, September 27, 1990

Kyle took a deep breath and held it. He was not used to the Chicago air. It tasted like rotting fish, and it burned his lungs.

His eyes scanned the alley to his left and right. The only movement he saw was a black and white cat as it jumped out of a dumpster at the far end. The cat approached a puddle left over from last night's storm and cautiously tasted it. A car drove by, and the cat jumped, then ran to safety behind the dumpster.

He returned his attention to the door in front of him. It was yellow and had chips in the paint, showing the previous colors of green, blue, and white. He didn't see a knob, or a handle, or any other way to open it from this side.

He gave three short, quick knocks. A few seconds passed before it opened, just enough for him to see a large, dark-skinned man standing on the other side. One of his arms alone was bigger than both of Kyle's, and he was at least a foot taller.

"Yeah?" His voice was deep. Kyle noticed a shimmer of gold in an otherwise mouthful of impressively white teeth, and a diamond earring adorned his left earlobe.

"I'm here to see Tony."

The man eyed Kyle, scrutinizing every inch. "Mister Lombardi ain't seeing no visitors today. Beat it." The door slammed, and Kyle heard the faint sound of a chain on the other side. He knocked again.

The door opened as far as the chain lock would allow. "I said get lost."

"I've come a long way to see Mister Lombardi."

The door slammed shut again.

He raised his voice, hoping it was enough to carry his message through the closed door. "Tell him I have news about his missing product."

The chain rattled against the inside of the door, and it opened wider this time, and Kyle finally got a good look at the man. He wore a short-sleeved, white and blue, vertical-striped button-down shirt. The top two buttons were undone, revealing a thick gold chain. The sleeves were stretched tight against his biceps.

If he were to flex, I bet there wouldn't be much left of that shirt.

In contrast, his black dress pants were loose-fitting.

The man stepped aside and motioned for him to enter. Kyle climbed the two stone steps and entered the building. His escort closed the door and led him down a hallway and through a bead-curtained door. He found himself in a large room that smelled of old sweat, cigarettes, and alcohol. To his left was a DJ booth. Directly in front of him, a stage jutted into the room, where several poles reached up from the floor to the ceiling.

He was led past some tables on his right and into a VIP area, where he saw a slightly overweight man seated in a red cushioned booth. Smoke drifted up from the cigar in his hand in thin wisps and lingered just above his head. There were stacks of cash and a few packages of a white substance wrapped in plastic on the table in front of him. His dark blue pinstripe suit looked tailor made. His hair was slicked back. He looked up at them as they approached.

71

"Boss," said the doorman. "You got a visitor."

"I told you I ain't seeing no one today."

"Says he's got news."

"News? What kind of news?"

The doorman glanced down at the table and nodded toward the white packages.

Kyle felt rough hands on him as the doorman patted him down.

"He's clean."

Tony pulled the cigar from his mouth and gently placed it in a green glass bowl. The large, diamond-encrusted gold ring on his pinky glimmered in the dim lighting. He waved them over, then motioned to an empty chair directly across from him. "Please, have a seat."

Tony waved his hand, and the doorman left.

"You'll need to forgive Junior. He's a little... protective."

Kyle sat in the chair. It was red, very soft, with thick cushions and armrests.

"Of course, that's what I pay him for. Can I offer you a drink, Mister...?"

"Lorne. Kyle Lorne. And no, thank you."

"So, tell me, Kyle Lorne, what's so important that you had to interrupt my day?"

"I'll get straight to it. I need your help."

Tony sat back, raised his arms, stretched them out, and rested them on the back of the red faux leather booth. "You need my help? With what?"

Kyle leaned forward. "A man claiming to be a cop, Jack, came to my town, chasing after a woman named Erica."

Tony's head cocked to the side.

"During my investigation…"

"Investigation?" Tony's hand dropped to his side. "You a cop?" His body seemed to tense up.

"I *was* a sheriff's deputy."

"Was?"

"I'm not anymore."

Tony relaxed. "What happened with that?"

"Jack happened. He killed one of my deputies, who was also a friend of mine. Then he shot someone else and stole my police cruiser. My boss didn't like that, so he fired me."

Tony reached for his cigar and slid it into his mouth. "Sounds like your boss is a dick."

Kyle grinned.

"Please, continue."

"As I told your associate…"

"Junior."

"As I told Junior, I know what happened to your missing product."

"And you're going to tell me out of the kindness of your heart?"

"Not exactly."

Tony took another pull on his cigar.

"I came to ask for a favor."

As the smoke drifted toward the ceiling, they formed tiny rings, reminding Kyle of mini donuts. The cigar smelled sweet, like oranges mixed with honeysuckle.

"What kind of favor?"

"The kind that I can't ask of anyone else."

Tony nodded. "You have my attention."

72

Serena turned the Cabriolet into the motel's parking lot, came to a stop under the blue and white sign, then climbed out and crossed the lot to the payphone just outside the office entrance. She dialed the number that she'd jotted down in her notebook and waited for someone to answer.

"Bristol Police Department, Sergent Pikeman."

"Sergeant Pikeman, it's Sheriff Rios. I'm here. I'm parked out front, under the sign."

"Okay. Officer Powell should be there in about five minutes."

"Thank you." She hung up the phone and glanced at her watch.

Five minutes. I can do that. It's not like I've never been on a stakeout before.

As a courtesy, she contacted the Bristol Police Department and informed them of her visit and the circumstances surrounding it. They'd been gracious enough to offer their help, which she gladly accepted. After her last run-in with Jack, she had no intention of taking him on by herself again. She was more worried about his safety, really, than hers. She was sure that next time, he'd walk away with more than just a broken nose.

If he walked away at all.

The motel was tan, with orange, blue, and brown accents.

Black metal numbers were screwed onto each of the sky-blue doors, and she located room 106 easily. It was the last one to her right, bottom floor.

There were three cars in the lot: a white Jeep Wagoneer with faux wood paneling parked outside of 101, a silver Lincoln Towncar at 103, and a maroon Honda Accord at 104. The spot in front of 106 was empty, and the curtains were closed.

A silver van drove past. The windows were blacked out, and she couldn't see anyone inside. It backed into the space just outside 106, then just sat there. There was no movement inside, and no one got out.

She started across the lot to her car and stopped short as a dark blue Jaguar XJ6 with Florida plates drove past.

She hurried back to the phone and slid a quarter into the slot.

Nathan answered on the second ring. "Millhaven sheriff's department. Deputy Rogers."

"Nathan."

"Serena. Everything okay?"

"Did you get any info on that license plate?"

"I did."

She heard papers rustling.

"It's registered to one Damian Martin, a Cuban national. Works at the Consulate in Miami. I ran the name through the database and got several hits. He's been on the FBI's radar for a few years, suspected of human trafficking, but he's never been charged."

"And now we have a name. Any word from North Carolina on that address I gave you?"

"They're putting a team together now. Should hear back within the hour."

"Good. I want to know the moment they call back."

"Of course." He paused. "Where did you say you got that intel from?"

"I didn't. But he's a solid source."

The Jaguar pulled into the spot next to the van. The rear doors opened, and Jack got out, followed by a well-dressed Hispanic man.

As they walked around the back of the car and toward the front of the van, Serena saw that the man in the suit had a gun pressed into Jack's side.

"I need to call you back." She ended the call before he could reply.

73

Serena watched as Jack was shoved into the back of the van, and the man in the suit slid the side door shut. He tucked his pistol into a shoulder holster underneath the suit jacket, snapped it shut, then turned toward room 106.

She saw the curtains flutter, then the door opened, and two large men stepped out. One of them was grasping the upper arm of a young girl. If she had to wager a guess, Serena would have said the girl was about eight years old. She had a yellow bow in her brown hair, and she was wearing what appeared to be a pink ballerina unitard with white stockings. She wasn't wearing shoes.

One man opened the back doors of the van while the other ushered the little girl inside.

Serena pulled her gun from its holster. "Hey!" She leveled the pistol at them as she ran toward the van.

The suit drew his weapon and fired a shot at her. It went wide and shattered the windshield of her car. She squeezed the trigger. The bullet ripped through the suit's upper shoulder, then punched a hole in the side of the van. He turned and dove into the passenger seat and slammed the door shut. The van's back wheels squealed with a puff of white smoke, and it lurched forward.

She saw the girl fall out of the van and roll on the ground as the vehicle sped off, the back doors swinging as it swerved out of the parking lot and onto the main road.

The second man reached for her.

Serena stopped running. "Don't!" She aimed her gun at him.

His eyes darted around the lot, then over his shoulder to the open door of room 106.

"On the ground, now!"

"No dispares. No dispares."

"En el suelo! On the ground! Now!"

He threw his hands high into the air and dropped to his knees.

She kept her gun trained on him as she moved forward. She glanced at the girl, now sitting with her knees to her chest, her arms wrapped around her legs. Her stockings had ripped, and blood was forming on her scraped knee. "Come here, sweetheart."

The girl was crying. She shook her head.

Serena unclipped her badge from her belt and held it up for her to see. "It's okay. I'm a cop. You can trust me."

The girl didn't move.

Serena looked back at the man and pointed to the ground. "En el suelo. Boca abajo. Face down."

He did as he was told.

"Arms out to your sides."

He reached his arms out to either side, and she cautiously got closer. When she was right on top of him, she clipped the badge back into place, pulled a pair of handcuffs from her back pocket, and secured his hands behind his back. She helped him roll over and sat him up.

"What's your name?" She asked the girl.

"Rachel."

"Rachel, I'm Serena. Can you tell me where you live?"

"I'm not supposed to talk to strangers."

Serena heard a car behind her and glanced over her shoulder as a Bristol City police cruiser stopped in the middle of the parking lot.

Rachel jumped up and ran to the officer as she got out of the car. She threw her arms around her leg and held on tight.

74

Kyle brushed a fingertip against the tabletop. It was smooth and cold. "I have files."

Tony leaned toward him. "What kind of files?"

"Case files."

"Comprised by whom?"

"My predecessor. The former sheriff of Millhaven."

"I met him a few times. Nice guy."

You met him more than just a few times.

"He was my dad."

"Well, ain't that some shit?"

Kyle nodded. "In his files, my dad said you're an honorable man. That despite your chosen... profession, you always keep your word, and you're loyal."

"That was kind of him."

"He also wrote that you and Armand don't exactly see eye to eye."

"Is that so?"

"He had proof that Armand was planning to run you out of business and take over as the main distributor on the East Coast."

Tony puffed on his cigar. "What proof?"

"I'm willing to share this information with you, but I need something in return."

"Do you?"

Kyle nodded.

"You're not sounding very cop-ish right now. Sounds like you're trying to gain my favor."

"That's because I am."

"So, tell me, Kyle Lorne. What is it you want?"

Kyle leaned forward. "First, I want this stuff out of my town." He motioned to the packages on the table.

Tony nodded. "And second?"

"We have a common interest."

"Which is?"

He took a breath. "I have reason to believe that Armand either killed my dad or had him killed."

Tony's eyes narrowed. "Is that so?"

Kyle nodded.

"So, my question remains. What is it you want from me?"

"I want you to help me get the proof that I need. Get him to admit what he did to my dad."

"And in return?"

He leaned forward. "In return, I'll help you get your product back."

If this surprised Tony, he didn't show it. "Are you sure you want to go down this path, Deputy?"

I'm not a deputy.

He nodded. "I've also recently discovered that Armand is involved in other endeavors." He took a breath. "Involving kidnapped children. This 'Jack' I mentioned, I know he works for you. He's in on that, too."

Tony's eyebrows raised. He gently placed the cigar back into the glass bowl. "Tread carefully."

"Erica found one of their stash houses. A storage locker in North Carolina. Jack told her where to find the key for it."

Tony exhaled. His eyes closed momentarily.

"You already knew, didn't you?"

"I suspected. Some Cubans approached me last year. Said they were interested in branching out from…" He waved his hand over the plastic-wrapped white powder on the table. "This. Said there was a lot of money in selling kids to countries overseas. I told them, in no uncertain terms, to go fuck themselves. I ain't into that." He picked up the cigar and rolled it between his fingers. He watched the red embers dance through the leaves and admired the smoke as it wafted upwards. "TJ said we should do it. 'Broaden our horizons,' as he put it."

"TJ?"

"You know him as Jack."

75

Tony leaned forward and picked up the glass in front of him. He slowly swirled the dark brown liquid, breathing in the aroma. "Detective Jack Pearce, the *real* detective Jack Pearce, weaseled his way into my business two years ago. I treated him like family. Last year, I found out he was a cop. When I confronted him about it, he had the stones to try to arrest me." He set the glass back onto the table. "I had TJ, Jack's foster brother, put a bullet in him."

"TJ."

Tony nodded. "Terrance Jenkins. He'd been working for me since he was a kid. Fifteen, I think. So anyway, Jack was trying to get him out of the business, put him on the straight and narrow. The thing is, TJ didn't want out. He was happy where he was. See, he never connected with his foster family. Always acted out. He was a good kid. Just needed to find his own way."

"Which led to a life of crime."

"Kid had been stealing his whole life. In and out of juvie. Then, one day, he tried to steal from me. Do you believe that? Tried to lift my wallet right out of my jacket pocket."

"How'd that work out?"

"I caught him in the act. But I was impressed with the balls on that kid. So, I peeled off a hundred bucks and offered him a job. Been with me ever since."

Kyle nodded.

"So anyway, after he popped that detective, TJ reached into his brother's coat, pulled out his badge and ID, and walked away. Just left him there to bleed out. A few days later, we were down at the docks, meeting with some guys from Peru. Things were starting to go south, and TJ, that crazy bastard, pulled that badge out and yelled, 'Chicago PD, everyone on the floor!'." He chuckled at the memory. "He handcuffed those guys, all five of them, and tossed them into the back of his car. We walked away with ten kilos of their product *and* our money. Later that night, he drove those poor bastards to an empty field in the middle of nowhere, poured gas all over the car, and threw a match at it. He stood there and watched it burn."

"Jesus."

"Right? Anyway, he's been using that badge ever since. But this is the first I've heard of him using it to convince an actual cop that he's a real detective. I gotta give it to him; that kid's got balls of steel."

Kyle sighed. "No one's ever found him out?"

"How could they? Everyone he arrests, let's just say they'll never be found. You can't talk if you're dead." He waved to Junior, who was still standing nearby. "I've got guys in your little town..."

"You have guys in Millhaven?"

Tony eyed him.

"Sorry. That's your business."

Tony nodded. "As I was saying, I got some guys there. I'll have them check in with TJ. If what you say is true, I'll take care of him myself. He's my responsibility, after all."

"And the mayor?"

"I'll do what I can to help with that, too. Kids are off-limits. But let me be clear, Kyle: if I get so much as a whiff that you're not being one hundred percent honest, or if you double-cross me..." He leaned toward Kyle, pulled a .45 pistol from the small of his back, and set it on the table. "Capiche?"

Kyle nodded. "Understood."

"Good."

Junior emerged with two plates of food and sat them down in front of them.

"Now, let's eat. I hope you like your steak rare."

76

Erica had hopped on the first flight out of Chicago and landed at Tri-Cities Airport just before noon. She took State Road 75 North to Blountville, then 394 East, toward Bristol Motor Speedway. From there, she turned north on 11E and took that into Bristol.

She was tired, and she couldn't wait to get back to her motel room and get some rest. Thankfully, the thirty-minute drive went quickly.

As she neared the motel, traffic crawled to a halt. When she finally came up to her turn, she noticed that the front parking lot was cordoned off with yellow police tape.

She passed the main entrance, turned left into the rear lot, and backed into the spot directly under her room on the second floor. Two empty spots over, a woman was loading suitcases into a blue sedan.

"What's going on?" She asked.

The woman slammed the trunk and eyed Erica. "There was a shootout this morning. Some perv tried kidnapping a little girl. Thankfully, an off-duty cop was here and stopped it. Some of them got away, though. The news has been here all day." She turned and disappeared into one of the rooms. Erica heard her speaking with someone else, a male, but she couldn't make out what they were saying.

She locked the Concord and strolled up the sidewalk toward the front of the building until she reached the yellow tape, then peered around the corner.

Several news vans lined the main road, with newscasters set up beside them, speaking into microphones. The parking lot itself was full of police cars. Three were from the local sheriff's department, four were from Bristol City Police, and two had Tennessee Highway Patrol markings. Outside the yellow tape, she also saw two completely blacked-out Chevy Suburbans.

FBI, maybe?

She leaned around the building and craned her neck in an attempt to see which room they were all interested in. Most of the crowd gathered around a car parked just a few feet from her.

"Erica?"

Startled out of her thoughts, she returned to the present, looked toward the voice, and saw Serena, the cop from Millhaven.

"Erica," Serena said again.

Erica turned and started back toward her car.

"Wait!"

She broke into a sprint, and as she rounded the corner, just within reach of the car, she ran head-first into a rather muscular man in a Tennessee Highway Patrol uniform.

77

"That's great news, Nathan. Thank you," Serena said into the phone.

"Yeah, it's a huge win for us. How's everything going in Bristol? You almost done?"

"Almost. I should be back by dinner." Serena watched Erica pacing inside the glass-walled interview room a few feet away.

"Have you heard from Kyle yet?" He asked.

"Not yet. He's probably at the airport now." She glanced at her watch. "He should be back in a few hours."

Erica now had her arms folded across her chest, staring directly at her. "I'll call back when I leave."

"Copy that, Boss."

"Nathan."

"Yeah, Boss?"

"Good work today."

"All I did was make a few phone calls. You did all the work."

She hung up the phone and crossed the room. An officer standing guard outside the interview room opened the door, and she nodded at him.

"Erica. Please, have a seat."

"I'll stand."

Serena nodded to the other officer in the room and sat in the chair beside him. "Curtis."

"Serena."

"Anything yet?"

He shook his head. "She hasn't said one word."

Erica turned to face them. "Am I under arrest?"

"That depends," Serena answered. "Do you have anything to

confess?"

Erica stared down at her.

Serena rested her hands on the table, one atop the other. "I know it was you who told Kyle about North Carolina."

"Yeah? So?"

"Local PD followed up. All those children are being reunited with their families as we speak."

Erica relaxed a little. "Seriously?"

Serena nodded. "Seriously. And it's all because of you."

Erica uncrossed her arms. She glanced down at the chair beside her, pulled it out, and lowered herself into it. "Good."

"What you did was brave. There are a lot of people who want to thank you."

Erica looked down at her hands. She started picking at her fingernails. "I'd like to remain anonymous if that's okay."

"Of course." She exchanged glances with Curtis. He nodded.

"Erica," he said, "you should know that we were able to save another little girl who went missing yesterday morning from Abingdon."

"Abingdon?"

Serena nodded. "She was at a rehearsal. She was still in her dance outfit when we found her."

"Jesus." Erica closed her eyes and flattened her hands on the table. "I was just there a few days ago. I was supposed to meet with Kyle."

This took Serena by surprise.

Is that where he disappeared to?

"You saw Kyle a few days ago?"

She shook her head. "I didn't get the chance. He never showed up. As I was leaving, Jack kidnapped me and took me to that old movie set in the mountains. Then he tied me to a chair. That's when that Cuban guy came in and threatened to kill me if I didn't get him a key."

Serena leaned forward.

Erica continued. "I told him it was in a storage locker in Chicago. Jack said my dad had another one in his office. Me and Jack went to get it, but you were already there. After you arrested him and left, I found it." She grinned. "That was a nice high kick, by the way. He deserved that."

"Yes, he did. You said he gave you twenty-four hours. That was three days ago. Did you see him again after that?"

"No. I'm good at hiding. When I went back to the motel this

morning, I thought he'd found where I was staying."

"Turns out Jack was staying there, too."

"No way."

"They were using his room as a pickup spot for that girl."

"Jesus."

Serena watched her face. Erica was genuinely surprised by this news. She pulled a pen from the slit in her shirt pocket and clicked it. She tapped the ballpoint against a notepad on the table in front of her. "I'd like to ask for your help."

"With what?"

"I have reason to believe that Armand, your dad, had something to do with the death of our former sheriff. Do you know anything about that?"

78

Serena fell onto the brown leather couch in Kyle's office. Bob and Nathan were coming in through the door behind her.

The cushions sighed as air escaped through the seams, and she sank into the soft material.

"How was the drive back?" Bob asked.

She'd left early this morning and drove straight to the station. She was exhausted and in desperate need of a shower. "Long."

"You should get some sleep."

"That's the plan. As soon as we're done here, I'm headed home."

Nathan strode past the couch and rounded the desk on the other side of the room. He placed his hands on the back of the sheriff's chair and raised his eyebrows in her direction, seeking her permission. She shrugged and nodded. He pulled the chair backward and lowered himself into it.

His face showed a hint of wonderment.

"It's comfortable, isn't it?"

"God, yes."

"It's yours if you want it."

He seemed to contemplate the thought, then shook his head. "I'm good, thanks."

"Don't blame you."

Bob leaned back on the desk and wriggled his rear onto the edge. "So, what's up, Boss? Why'd you call me in on my day off?"

She pulled the black scrunchie from her ponytail and lifted the ball cap from her head. Her wavy black hair fell to her shoulders.

She examined the front of the hat, visually tracing the outline of the

175

letters that spelled the word "SHERIFF" before gently setting it next to her on the couch. Then she returned her attention to her two deputies. "Kyle's gotten himself into something, and he's gonna need our help finding his way out."

Nathan leaned forward on the desk. "What kind of something?"

Bob shifted toward her as well.

She placed her elbows on her knees and planted her feet flat on the floor. "Those kids we saved? The anonymous tip I got? That was him."

"No shit," Bob said.

"No shit." She realized her fingers were clasped so tightly together that they were turning white. She pulled her hands apart and gently shook them to get the blood flowing.

"What's going on?" Nathan asked.

"That missing person we've been looking for from the inn..."

Nathan nodded. "Erica Hawthorne."

She nodded.

Bob stood. "Wait. What? Erica Hawthorne? Like in Mayor Armand Hawthorne?"

She met his gaze. "Yeah. As in Mayor Armand Hawthorne. She's his daughter."

"How the hell did that happen?"

She noticed the smile on Nathan's face when he answered.

"Later, you and me can sit down over a cold beer, and I'll tell you all about where babies come from."

Bob shot him a look.

"Guys, focus."

They returned their attention to her.

"I found some files at Kyle's house that his dad left behind."

They both nodded in unison. She didn't think that either of them realized they were doing it.

"What kind of files?" Nathan asked.

She took a breath. "Personal files that he kept on an investigation he was conducting into the mayor."

"The mayor?" Bob said. "He seems to be the center of a lot of conversations lately."

She nodded. "Henry was undercover, on his own, gathering intel."

"Investigating what?"

"Apparently, our mayor is involved with a drug distribution ring out of Chicago."

"No shit?" Nathan asked.

"Holy crap," Bob said.

She nodded. "From what I read, Henry thought Armand was onto him. A few days later, he was dead."

Nathan's eyebrows raised. "Do you think it could have been a coincidence?"

"I don't believe in those. Everything happens for a reason." She studied her fingers for a moment, then picked at the pink polish on her thumb. "I had a chat with Erica last night with Bristol PD. Without revealing anything to her, I did get her to verify some things."

"Oh?" Nathan asked.

She nodded. "I think she knows something, but she's either too scared to say, or she's hiding something."

"What kind of something?" Nathan asked.

"I don't know." She met his gaze. "But we need to find out. Kyle has been poking around in this mess, too. We need to make sure he doesn't end up like his dad."

79

"She asked you what?"

Erica hated repeating herself. She pulled the phone away from her ear long enough to slide a beige cashmere sweater over her head and slip her arm through the sleeve. "I said she asked if I knew anything about you being involved in Sheriff Lorne's death."

"Why would she ask you that?"

She sighed. "I don't know, Dad. Maybe because she suspects you had something to do with it?"

"What did you tell her?"

"I didn't rat you out if that's what you're asking."

"You know I didn't have anything to do with that, don't you? His cause of death was a heart attack."

"She seems to think otherwise."

The line was quiet for a moment. "Did she say why?"

"She didn't specify, no. She said she found new evidence to suggest that he was murdered."

She gave her reflection in the full-length mirror a once over, twisting to each side as she admired her new sweater.

"Murdered? How's that possible?"

She raised the cuff to her mouth and grasped the plastic fastener with her teeth. "She apparently thinks it's possible," she said with a mouthful of price tag. She jerked her arm away, and the plastic snapped in two.

"What was that?"

She *patoo'ed* the tag toward the wastebasket, missing the mark by about a foot. She sighed. "I said she apparently thinks it's possible."

She heard a faint beep.

178

"Crap," he said. "I need to take this. I'll call you back."

The line went dead before she could respond.

She cradled the receiver long enough for the line to reset, then raised it back to her ear and jabbed the numbers on the phone. She counted three rings before someone answered.

"Diga."

She frowned. "Why do you always sound so angry when you answer the phone?"

"It's one of my endearing qualities." His Cuban accent was thick.

"I believe that." She cradled the phone between her shoulder and her ear while she stepped into a pair of jeans. "I'll be there in fifteen minutes."

"He's not alone."

"Doesn't matter."

"What if he doesn't agree?"

"I have other buyers lined up." She waited for a reply. None came. "How's our guest? Is he comfortable?"

"He was complaining about the lack of amenities. I don't know why I can't just kill him and be done with it."

"We still need him. For now."

The line was silent.

"Remember our deal. I know you and Jack had your differences when you worked for Tony, but you work for me now. If you can't follow orders, I'll find someone who can."

He grunted.

"I'm serious. Don't do anything yet."

"Fine. I'll see you in fifteen minutes."

80

Kyle surveyed the diner, looking for the one face he'd hoped to see.

"She isn't here today, Sheriff."

He glanced toward the voice and saw Ethel heading his way. Her hair, a mix of white with remnants of dark brown, was piled high on her head in a 60s-style beehive. He wasn't sure how old she was, but he knew she looked the same today as when she was his fifth-grade teacher - right down to the same shade of eyeliner.

She peered at him over the top of her horn-rimmed glasses. "Go ahead and sit wherever you want."

He went to the back and slid into his booth, not realizing she was one step behind him. She slapped a menu onto the table, taking him by surprise.

"Is she okay? She usually works Friday mornings."

Ethel scowled. "Lauren? She's fine. That no good ex of hers left her high and dry again; it was his turn to take Molly to school. I'm working her shift, and she'll be in tonight to cover mine."

He nodded.

She dug her fingers into the side of her hair and, like a magician, plucked a pen from it while pulling a notepad from the pocket of her apron. "What can I get started for you?"

"Just coffee. Black."

She looked hurt. "Just coffee? You sure?"

He nodded. "Just coffee. Thanks."

Her head tilted to the side, and her eyes narrowed. After a few breaths, she stabbed the pen back into her hair and shoved the notepad into her pocket. She turned, crossed the few feet to the kitchen, and pushed through the door.

As she went, Kyle thought he heard her mumble something about a "cheap tipper."

Movement outside on the sidewalk caught his attention. He glanced up to see Serena standing there, staring at his Jeep. If the window wasn't there to separate them, he could have reached out and touched her.

She turned and met his gaze. He smiled and nodded.

She nodded back, then found her way to the entrance.

A few seconds later, she was sitting across from him. "We need to talk."

"Good morning. You want something to eat? Coffee?"

She took a quick look around the diner before turning back. "Where's your girlfriend?"

"If you're referring to Lauren, she's not here."

"I see." She seemed distracted.

He leaned toward her and folded his arms on the table. "Okay. What gives?"

"Hmm?"

"You have something on your mind. What is it?"

Her hands dropped to her lap, and she stared into his eyes. "What were you doing in Chicago?"

81

Erica strolled past a tour bus that advertised everlasting life with Jesus Christ and passed through a set of revolving doors. Glancing to her left, she saw that the hotel restaurant was serving breakfast, and the dining area was filled with guests.

She found the person she was looking for and weaved through the patrons, making it to her destination without actually bumping into anyone, which was a feat in itself.

As she pulled a chair away from the table and lowered herself into it, she examined the faces of the three men seated around it. "What's good here?"

When Damian recognized her, his mouth curled into a snarl. "You're too brave for your own good. Do you have my key?"

She frowned and shook her head. "Afraid not."

Damian picked up a cloth napkin, wiped it against his mouth, then set it on the table and neatly folded it into a square. "That's too bad. I told you what would happen if you didn't get it to me. I even gave you extra time." He nodded to the man to his right, seated directly to her left.

The man stood.

She casually glanced up at him. "Sit down."

"Excuse me?" Damian asked.

She grinned as the man standing behind Damian pulled a pistol from his waistband, draped a white napkin over it, and pressed the muzzle against the back of his head.

"The lady said sit."

Erica smiled. "I'm sorry. Where are my manners? This is Paolo. Paolo, meet Damian."

Paolo nodded. "Hola."

Damian waved his hand toward the chair, and the man returned to his seat. He glanced over his shoulder at Paolo. "I know you. You're one of Tony's men."

"I was."

He turned back to Erica. "You have some nerve coming here like this."

"I know. My dad always said I wasn't too bright."

"He was right."

She reached across the table, plucked an olive from his salad, and popped it into her mouth. She gave a side-eye glance to the man on her right. "I don't know you. Leave."

The man looked to Damian for guidance. Damian gestured for him to stay.

She shifted her gaze to the stranger and stared into his eyes. "Leave now, or get a bullet in your head."

Paolo raised his other hand and pointed a second, equally concealed pistol at him.

He rose from the table and disappeared into the crowd without a word.

"What now?" Damian asked.

"Now, we talk."

"And what, perchance, should we talk about?"

She placed her elbow on the table and rested her chin in her hand. "Why don't we discuss the deal we're about to make?"

He laughed. "Deal? What deal?"

"The one where you and I cut my father out of the picture and go into business for ourselves."

82

Damian placed his thumb on the edge of the plate and pushed it away. "And what makes you think I'd go into business with you? You're nada."

She grinned. "You have no idea who I am."

"I know you're a scared little girl."

She tried, and failed, to suppress the chuckle that found its way out. "Are you referring to this?" Her finger brushed against the days-old cut on her cheek.

He smiled as he lifted a glass, tipped it in her direction, and then sipped at the clear liquid. She could barely hear the ice clink through the laughter that erupted on the far side of the dining area.

"Don't underestimate me. You'll be sorely disappointed."

"Tell me," he set the glass back onto the table. "What would your father say if he found out?"

"He won't."

"What makes you so sure? I might tell him myself."

"Trust me, it's the last thing he's worried about right now."

"Is that so?"

She nodded.

"And why's that?"

"Let's just say he has more pressing matters to worry about."

"Such as?"

She feigned a yawn. "I'm tired of this back and forth. Are we going to talk business, or am I wasting my time?"

"If those are my only choices, I'd go with… you're wasting your time."

She smiled. "And this is your final answer? You don't want to think

184

about it?"

"There's nothing to think about. As I said, you're nothing. And I'm going to kill you the first chance I get."

She pushed her chair backward and rose. She stared down at him for an instant before rounding the table to stand beside him.

He looked up at her.

She leaned down and put her lips close to his ear. "I wouldn't count on that."

"You're already dead, cabrona. You just don't..."

The skin on his neck gave little resistance as the steak knife pierced through and sliced through his carotid artery.

She grabbed a handful of his hair and gently lowered his head to the table, then kneeled and stared into his horror-filled eyes. "I'm sorry. That was rude of me. Were you saying something?" She wasn't certain, but she thought she actually saw his life slowly drift away. "Fascinating."

Beside her, Paolo tucked the pistols into his waistband. "I hope you know what you're doing."

She glanced around the room. Surprisingly, everyone was too involved in their own conversations to notice that a man was just killed less than ten feet away from them. Paolo offered her the cloth napkin, and she draped it over Damian's head. "Let's go."

83

Kyle leaned back as Ethel set a cup of steaming coffee on the table. "I had business there."

"What kind of business could you possibly have in Illinois?"

He studied Serena's face, trying to gauge what she already knew. He lifted his cup and gently blew over the rim, redirecting the steam as it rose from the dark liquid. "You know... business."

She scooted forward and leaned toward him. "Did it have anything to do with Tony Lombardi?"

His cup froze halfway from the table to his lips.

Dammit, Serena.

But then, it didn't surprise him. She was the smartest person he knew. If anyone was going to figure it out... "Where did you hear that name?"

"So, yes. You met with a drug lord. Care to share what you two talked about?"

"Not really."

She sighed, then sat back in the booth.

He raised the cup and gently sipped the hot drink as she dug into her pocket. Her hand re-emerged, grasping a piece of folded paper, which she slapped onto the table between them.

"What's that?"

Her eyes never left his as she tilted her head toward it, inviting him to have a look.

He set the cup back on the table, then placed the tip of his finger on the paper and slid it closer.

For an instant, he admired the clean, crisp edges of the folds. He opened the paper.

How in the hell…?

"Where did you get this picture?"

"Really? That's the first thing that comes to mind?"

He re-folded the photocopy of the image of his dad, standing next to Armand Hawthorne and Tony Lombardi. "Serena."

"I'll ask you again: what were you doing in Chicago?"

"How much do you know?"

Her head tilted to the side. "Does that matter? Why don't we start with what *you* know? And why you didn't think it was important enough to tell me?"

"You saw my dad's files."

She nodded. "I saw your dad's files."

"So, you already know everything I do."

"Do I? How long have you been digging into this?"

"Six months. Since I cleaned out my dad's house and found them in his garage."

"Six months? And not once did it ever occur to you to let me know what's going on?"

He shrugged. "An oversight on my part."

She nodded. "To say the least."

He took a breath and held it.

It would be nice to have a confidant in all of this.

"As you might have surmised, my dad knew about Armand's side business."

She nodded. "Drug smuggling."

"Distribution, but yeah. He managed to find his way into the inner circle, I guess you could call it, and gained Armand's trust. So much so that Armand introduced him to Tony."

"According to your dad's reports, he was trying to get enough information to take to the FBI."

He nodded. "Right. But along the way, he also found out that Armand was hiking up his prices and not telling Tony about it. Basically, stealing from him."

She nodded.

"Dad went back to Tony and showed him proof of what he found, and Tony took care of it."

"Took care of it how?"

"I don't know. I can't find any information on that. But from then on, Dad spent a lot of time in Chicago. I think he might have been working with the FBI at that point. Undercover or something. Maybe gathering info? I don't know. He didn't keep any records of that. But then I came across another file, where he wrote about Armand 'branching out' from trafficking drugs to something involving a Cuban national. That was his last entry. According to the date on that one, he died a week later."

84

Serena's mind was processing what he'd just said. "Are you telling me you think *Armand* killed your dad?"

Kyle nodded as he shrugged. "I think so, yeah."

"Because of whatever he found involving that Cuban national?"

"That's my working theory."

"Yesterday, when you called me, I was following up on a lead that took me to Bristol."

"Bristol? Tennessee or Virginia?"

"Tennessee. Abingdon locals had found Leo's car in a parking lot up there. The one that Jack stole after he..." She took a breath. "There was a key in the trunk. Turned out it was for a motel in Bristol. So, I went and checked it out. Jack was there."

"Jack? Is that where he was staying?"

She shrugged. "I didn't get a chance to ask. I also had a run-in with a Cuban national. Nathan had run the plates on his car before that..."

"Before that?"

She nodded. "That's another story entirely. Did you know that Arnie is a genius?"

"Oh?"

"Remind me later. I'll tell you about that one."

He nodded. "Okay. The Cuban?"

"Right. Damian Martin. Diplomat with the Cuban embassy."

"No shit?" He leaned onto the table.

"I think he was holding Jack hostage. I can't be sure. But they were trying to kidnap a little girl. There's no telling what would've happened to her if I wasn't there."

"Jesus."

She nodded. "Rachel. She's home with her parents now. We arrested one suspect. Jack, Damian, and at least two others got away."

"I didn't know. Are you okay?"

"I'll live. My car took the brunt of it."

"The suspect you arrested. Did he say anything?"

She shook her head. "Nada. He's not talking. Like, literally. Won't say a word. Bristol has him in custody until his arraignment Monday morning."

His eyes closed, and he pinched the bridge of his nose. "What the hell is going on?"

She shrugged. "That's the burning question, isn't it?"

He nodded.

"Here's another one for you: what's our next move?"

His head tilted to the side, and he met her gaze. "*Our* next move?"

"Well, yeah. You can't possibly think I'm gonna let you do this by yourself?"

"That was the plan."

"No offense, but that plan sucks."

"No argument here."

Her radio hissed. "Sheriff, it's Nathan."

She unclipped it from her belt and raised it. "Go ahead."

"We just got a call from the locals in Johnson City. They responded to a restaurant where a man was killed in the middle of a crowded room."

She sighed. "And they called us, why?"

"They found the vic's car in the parking lot. It matched the BOLO we put out on that Cuban, so they faxed over a photo for us to verify. Boss, their vic was Damien Martin."

85

"So, what does that mean?" Bob asked.

They were in the conference room at the Sheriff's station. Kyle was sitting across from Bob. Nathan was on his right, and Serena was pacing along the wall behind him. He glanced up at her when she answered.

"It means we don't have a case anymore."

"So that's it? It's all done?" Bob's face matched his tone: he wasn't happy. And with good reason.

She stopped pacing briefly. "Damian Martin *was* a person of interest by way of being linked with Jack. He was involved in a kidnapping case that started in Bristol and ended in North Carolina. The FBI swooped in and took over that one. Then, he was found dead in a restaurant in Johnson City. All of those places are out of our jurisdiction. So yeah, it looks like that's it as far as he goes." She pulled a vacant chair from under the table and lowered herself into it. "But this is far from over. Jack is still out there, and we still have our mayor to deal with."

"And Erica," Nathan chimed in.

Kyle leaned in on the table. "We don't have any hard evidence to arrest either of them, and God only knows where Jack is."

Erica nodded. "You're right. Plus, we don't know if Erica actually had anything to do with John Doe's death at the hospital. All we know for certain is that she was in the room when he died. And as far as Mayor Hawthorne, we have Henry's files and notes, but without his testimony to back it all up, we don't have enough to take to the State Police and get a warrant."

"So, what do we do?" Bob asked.

Kyle glanced at Serena as she looked up at him. "You're the sheriff. I'm just a civilian now. It's your call."

She nodded. "Right." She took a slow breath. "We keep looking for Jack. There's got to be a way to trace where he's been. If we can do that, maybe we can figure out where he's going. I find it hard to believe that he drove all the way here from Bristol every day. He had to have been staying someplace local."

Bob and Nathan nodded.

"And Hawthorne?" Nathan asked.

"I can't legally use any of our resources to investigate a prominent figure like the town mayor."

Kyle grinned. "If only you knew someone outside the department who you knew you could trust."

"If only."

He rose from his chair. "I'll keep you updated."

"That would be a pleasant change."

He frowned at her.

She smiled.

"What about us?" Bob asked.

"With everything that's happened, has anyone had a chance to look at that car Kyle found at Beverly's?"

Nathan glanced over at Bob, who shook his head.

"Get ahold of Andy. Have him bring it over in the morning. Put it in the yard out back. Then go over every inch of it and let me know what you find."

Nathan rose from the table. "Copy that, Boss."

86

Erica smacked her lips together, evenly distributing the ChapStick, and adjusted the rear-view mirror.

Paolo sat beside her, gazing into the passenger mirror on his right. "Which one is it?"

She rubbed the tip of her pinky over her bottom lip, smoothing out the beeswax coating. "Pink jacket."

He quickly searched through the gathering of parents and their children waiting to cross the street behind them. "Ah. Got it."

He watched as a blonde woman stepped into the crosswalk, holding onto the hand of a young girl in a pink jacket; a bright, lime green backpack bounced against her back. "How do you want to do this?"

She dropped the small yellow tube into a tray under the radio. It rattled against a few coins and a transparent red Bic lighter. "We wait until they turn the corner. When they're out of sight, we grab them."

"Right. You want them in the trunk?"

She shot him a sideways glance. "Savage. But no. The girl can ride in the back with you. The mom will be up here with me."

He nodded.

"You ready?"

"Ready."

She slid the shifter into drive, lifted her foot from the brake pedal, and the car crept forward. She drove the long way around the block, and now the woman and the girl were in front of them, walking up the sidewalk toward them.

She pulled to the curb and stopped the car two houses away. Paolo pushed the door open and climbed out. He turned back and leaned in through the window.

She checked the mirror. "Wait."

They were now one house away.

"Wait."

Twenty feet. Fifteen. Ten. They passed the front fender.

"Now."

Paolo twisted and grabbed the girl's upper arm.

"HEY!" she shouted.

The woman turned and swung her purse at him, then froze when she noticed his gun.

He motioned with his head toward the front seat. "Get in."

The woman stared at him, seemingly uncertain of what to do.

"Now."

She did as she was told.

Paolo opened the back door, pushed the girl inside, and climbed in behind her.

"Please," the woman said. "I don't have any money."

"Close the door," Erica said.

"Mommy?" the girl said.

The woman looked over her shoulder into the back seat. "It's okay, Molly. It'll be okay."

"Door," Erica said. "Please."

The woman closed the door. "What do you want?"

Erica glanced back at the mirror and waited while Paolo fastened the seatbelt around Molly's waist. "Ready?"

He nodded. "Ready."

87

Saturday, September 29, 1990

The storm, if it could be called that, had come and gone without a single drop anywhere in Millhaven. The dark clouds had given way to clear blue skies, leaving dainty wisps of white streaks overhead.

Kyle felt cheated. Being among the minority of humans on the planet, he actually enjoyed the rain. The sound of wet drops hitting the ground, the gentle, quiet roar as they fell. He felt at peace during those moments, no matter what else was going on.

He clipped the translucent blue water bottle to his belt, latched the Jeep's tailgate, and took a deep breath. The morning air was cool and crisp, and he felt it fill his lungs.

He glanced at the watch wrapped around his left wrist. 6:05 a.m. The tiny icon below the numbers informed him that the sun would rise in twenty-five minutes. That gave him plenty of time to get to his favorite spot, where he would have the perfect view as it slowly crept out from behind the mountain range to the east.

He turned away from the Jeep as he pulled the zipper on his windbreaker. It wasn't especially cold this morning, but he didn't want to leave it behind, only to need it later. In his experience, it was always coldest just before dawn.

As he moved toward the edge of the field, he listened as the world around him awakened. Nearing the path, he quickened his pace, and by the time he passed the crooked tree that marked the start of the trail, he was at a full jog.

He'd decided to run his route backward this morning to give himself a bit of a challenge. By the time he'd made the complete circuit, he'd finish by running uphill instead of the usual flat, level terrain. He didn't have a reason for this change; he just felt like doing it.

He knew, however, that he'd probably regret that decision later.

As he ran, his thoughts, as always, turned to his work, even though he was currently unemployed.

Maybe I'll start my own business.

Doing what? What skills do you have?

I don't know. Maybe private investigator?

PI? In Millhaven? Do you really want to get paid to dig into your friends' lives? How long would that last?

True. Maybe someplace else? Bristol? Johnson City? Hell, there's nothing tying me down. I could move to another state. Start all over. Someplace where no one knows me. Where I don't know anyone.

You could. But a private investigator? *That's not a very noble or lucrative profession.*

He leaped over a small fallen branch. To his left, through the trees, the sky was a dark, dull red.

The path twisted to the right. He cut the corner a little short, and his arm brushed against the bark of a cypress.

I've always thought about taking flying lessons. Maybe I could do that. There's that university that offers a two-year program for commercial pilot.

Then what? Are you going to sit in a closet-sized box and be a glorified taxi driver?

Tuning out his thoughts, he focused on the rocky terrain. He was nearing the edge of the forest where the path turned into the mountainside. Over the years, he'd responded to too many calls of hikers not paying attention in this area and finding themselves at the bottom of the mountain.

None of them had survived.

He gradually slowed to a walk. In front of him, miles away, the sun was kissing the sky over the east mountain range. He was amazed, as he always was, as the brilliant reds, oranges, and yellows slowly overtook the previous night's darkness.

88

Erica pushed through the wooden half-doors and glanced around the room at the bar, the stairs, and the old piano.

In the center of the room, fifteen feet away, was Jack. She saw that he had a bruised and swollen left eye and dried blood along the side of his face, originating from his right ear.

He pulled against the thin rope that bound him to the chair. His biceps flexed through the dark blue t-shirt; his hands were tied behind him. "I'm gonna kill you."

"You're not the first person to say that, you know. Didn't end well for the last guy."

His breathing was heavy. "What do you want?"

"It wasn't that long ago that I was sitting right where you are now, asking you that very same question." She cautiously moved closer. "What do I want? Let me start with what I *didn't* want. I *didn't* want to be threatened. I *didn't* want my face to be cut. Oh, and I *definitely* didn't want to be beaten up in a bus station bathroom."

"That was business."

She nodded. "Of course it was. Just like *this* is business."

"You stole from me. You stole from Mister Lombardi. We couldn't let that go."

"We had a deal, Jack. Do you remember that?"

He looked away.

"You promised to help me get my dad out of the way. You promised you'd help me take over his business."

He nodded. "I know."

"What happened? Did you grow a conscience?"

He shook his head.

"No? Then what?"

"It was those kids. I told you; I won't do nothin' that hurts kids. That's wrong."

Her brows furrowed. "You hurt kids every day with that crap you sell. Different method, same outcome."

"The hell it is. You want to kidnap them. Sell them into slavery against their will. The people who use my stuff, they chose to do that."

She shrugged. "Potato, potahdo. Here's the deal. You're gonna honor your promise. You're gonna help me get rid of my dad, once and for all."

He tilted his head and met her gaze. "Am I?"

"You are."

"Or what? You gonna kill me?"

"No, not you."

The doors swung open behind her.

"Daddy!"

Erica grabbed Molly's arm, stopping her from running across the room. She maneuvered the girl closer to him but kept her just out of reach.

"Baby girl! You okay?"

Molly nodded. "I'm fine. They didn't hurt me. Are you okay? You look hurt."

He glared at Erica. "Don't you touch her."

She smiled. "I'm not gonna hurt her. I'm not a monster." She grabbed the back of a nearby chair with her free hand, pulled it from under an old table, and swung it around. She guided Molly into it, facing her father. "Besides, I have other plans for this precious little girl." She pulled a length of cord from her pocket and tied Molly's hands behind her, fastening the restraints to the wood dowels of the chair's back. "Paolo!"

Behind her, the half-doors squeaked as Paolo pushed through them, pulling Lauren behind him.

"TJ!" Lauren yelled.

A tear escaped from the corner of Jack's one good eye and slid down his cheek. "Tell me what you want."

"Not much. Just my dad in jail. Or dead. I don't care which."

89

Serena squinted in the morning sun as she stepped onto the deck. The air was cool and refreshing. She brought a mug to her lips, one hand holding the handle, the other cupped around the opposite side, and sipped the warm coffee.

Her oversized gray Boston Redsox t-shirt gently waved in the breeze, causing the bottom hem to tickle the back of her legs, just above her knees.

She reached down and rubbed the tingles away, then pushed a leaf aside with her toe. She leaned against the wood railing and looked out over the treetops.

The sun was high over the mountains in the distance, and the sky looked like it was on fire.

What's that saying? Red sky in the morning, something about a warning?

She hoped it wasn't an omen.

She closed her eyes, took a slow, deep breath, and held it.

A hawk screeched somewhere nearby and was answered by another somewhere farther away.

She glanced over her shoulder to check the time on the microwave in the kitchen, just inside the sliding glass doors.

8:45. I wonder if Andy dropped the car off yet.

She gave another look at the scenery, then went back inside, setting the mug on the kitchen counter as she walked past and headed toward the back of the house. As she approached the bedroom, she grabbed the collar of the shirt, pulled it over her head, and tossed it onto the bed.

Almost an hour later, showered, dressed, with her damp hair tied into a loose ponytail and a toasted Eggo waffle hanging from her mouth, she pressed the wallphone receiver to her ear and dialed the sheriff's station.

Nathan answered. "Morning, Boss."

"Good morning, Nathan. Did you guys get hold of Andy?"

"We did. He said he can have the car here by 10:30."

She nodded. "Sounds good. I'll be headed into town in a bit to run some errands, so I'll be nearby if you need me."

"Appreciate that, Boss, but it's your day off. Try to enjoy it."

"I'm not even sure what that means anymore, but I'll do my best." Her phone beeped. "Thanks, Nathan. I'll call you later. Let me know if you find anything." She tapped the hookswitch to accept the new call. "Hello?"

"Sheriff." It was Armand Hawthorne.

"Mayor?"

"Sheriff, you need to get here now. Someone is trying to break into my house."

90

Erica held the gun steady as she leveled it at him. "Put the phone down, dad."

"Erica, think about this."

"I have thought about it. A lot." She motioned to the phone with the pistol. "Put the phone down."

Armand did as he was told.

"Who did you call?"

He silently stared at her.

"I'm not going to ask you again."

"I called the sheriff. She's on her way."

She smiled and glanced over her shoulder. "This is too perfect." She nodded toward Paolo and then toward the chair in the corner of the room. "Put him over there."

Paolo dragged Jack across the room and lowered him into the seat.

Armand was intently watching. "What the hell are you doing? Is he dead?"

Erica shrugged. "I don't really know. Paolo, is he dead?"

Paolo brought his index finger to Jack's neck and pressed it against an artery. "Not yet."

She turned back to Armand. "That's somewhat disappointing." She tilted her head and motioned toward the chair next to Armand. "Have a seat."

He sat.

"Is Mary home? She should join us."

"No. She went to the market."

"Shame. How much time do we have until she gets back?"

"It's an all-day thing with her. She'll be gone until around noon."

She nodded. "Well. We can't wait that long."

"What do you want?" His eyes shifted from her to Jack, then back.

"Why is everyone so concerned with what I want? I mean, why now? No one ever cared before this week. It was always 'Shut up, Erica,' 'This is none of your concern, Erica,' 'Mind your own business, Erica.'"

She could see the look of concern on his face.

"Nothing? No answer?" She gave a sideways nod and glanced over at Paolo. "Are we ready?"

He nodded. "Yep."

She turned back to Armand. "Here's what's going to happen. Jack over there came to see you to discuss… whatever the hell it is you guys talk about. He didn't like what you had to say, and he pulled a gun on you. You had no choice but to shoot him."

She turned and fired a round into Jack's chest.

Armand jumped to his feet. "Jesus!"

She turned back to him. "Daddy, you know better. That's blasphemy."

"Erica…"

"Anyway. Before he died, Jack got off a shot of his own."

Armand's eyes grew wide. He held his hands up, palms facing her. "Wait."

Paolo brought his pistol up and aimed it at Armand.

"Please. Don't do this. We can figure it out. We can…"

Paolo pulled the trigger, and Armand fell back into his leather chair.

She watched as blood leaked from the tiny red hole in his chest and soaked into his white cashmere sweater.

"You okay?" Paolo asked.

"Why wouldn't I be?"

"He's your dad."

She held her pistol out for him. "He was a sperm donor."

He took the gun from her and wiped it down with a cloth that he'd retrieved from his pocket.

She glanced at Armand, then turned and left the room. "Set it up. Call me when it's done."

He nodded.

91

Kyle placed the empty water bottle on the passenger seat and slid the key into the ignition. With a quick twist, the engine came to life.

With the windows down, he took his time getting back to the main road, enjoying the weather, the scenery, and the peace and quiet along the way.

I could sell the house and buy a nice little spot on a lake. Maybe open up a little fishing resort, rent out boats, camping cabins.

Okay. I can't argue with that one. I should look into that.

Half an hour later, as he rounded the last curve before the road, he saw a black four-door Suburban blocking the exit. The tinted windows were up, concealing whoever was inside.

He gently pressed his foot onto the brake pedal, and the Jeep slowed to a stop.

The truck's rear passenger-side door opened, and a well-dressed man in a three-piece suit stepped out.

Lombardi? What's he doing out here?

He shut off the car, unclipped the seatbelt, and climbed out.

Tony took a step toward him. "It's about fucking time. I've been waiting almost an hour."

Kyle cautiously approached the SUV. "What's going on?"

"Get in. We need to talk."

"Is everything okay?"

He motioned to the open door. "Please. I feel like I'm gonna be eaten alive by a swarm of chiggers standing out here." He reached up, slapped his neck, and examined his open palm.

Kyle scanned the inside of the truck before climbing in. Lombardi motioned for him to scoot over, then sat on the edge of the seat, swung his legs in, and pulled the door closed. "Kyle, we have a problem and I thought it was best to tell you face-to-face."

"Okay."

"I had my guys check in on TJ like I said I would. It took them a while to track him down. He's a slippery son of a bitch. When they did, I was less than thrilled by what they found."

"Which was?"

"I promised you I'd take care of him if what you said was true. Let's leave it at that."

He nodded. "Okay."

"It seems, however, that in the short time it took me to get down here, they lost him."

"Oh?"

"This girl you spoke of, Erica. I do know her. During our last meeting, I couldn't remember, but when I saw a couple of photographs, it came back to me. She's the mayor's daughter. She came to see me one night and tried to convince me to help her take over her dad's business. Kept saying she could make me rich beyond my imagination."

Kyle stayed silent, taking everything in.

"Anyway. My guys, they found her and TJ, only she had him tied up. Looked like they beat the shit out of him, too."

"Where was this?"

Tony held the cigar a few inches from his face. He stared at it as if waiting for it to do something. Finally, he turned and looked at Kyle. "Some backwoods, old west, cowboy, hick town saloon. You believe that shit? I knew this place was in the middle of fucking nowhere, but come on. An old west saloon? The fuck is that all about?"

Kyle considered explaining the concept of TV and movie filming locations but decided against it.

"My guys had to leave the area to find a phone. By the time they got back, they were gone."

"She took him someplace else?"

"Hey, you're pretty good. You should be a cop or something."

He frowned. "Any idea where they went?"

Tony shook his head. "They're out there looking now."

Kyle nodded. "Thank you."

"I don't need thanks. I need my product. Don't you forget about our deal."

"I remember."

"Good. Now get the fuck outta my car. I need to go take a shower and get all this nature bullshit off me."

92

As Serena pulled into the driveway, she noticed the front door was wide open. "I'm pulling up now. How far are you?"

It was difficult to hear Bob over his siren wailing in the background. "Five minutes. Nathan is two minutes out. You waiting or going in?"

"I'm going in. Call out when you get here."

"Copy that."

She parked behind the Mazarati, jumped out, and shoved the radio into her back pocket, then hurried to the open front door. "Millhaven Sheriff's Department!"

There was no answer.

She put her back to the door and pulled the PPK from the holster in her jeans pocket, her thumb instinctively pulling the hammer rearward. "I'm coming in!"

Holding the gun close, she cleared the dining room and then moved to the living room while scanning the top of the stairs.

She noticed that Armand's office door was closed. "Mayor Hawthorne, you in there?"

She inched closer and pressed up against the wall beside the door.

"Armand? It's Serena. Are you okay?"

She pushed the door open slowly and peered into the room.

Armand was in the chair behind his desk; his head was tilted backward, and his sweater was soaked with blood.

"Armand!"

She opened the door and entered the room, pointing the pistol toward the blind corner and aiming at the person in the chair next to the lamp.

Jack.

His eyes were closed, and he wasn't moving.

Slowly, she moved closer, her eyes locked onto the pistol lying on his right leg. When she was close enough, she reached out, grabbed the gun, then quickly stepped back. She tossed it onto the floor on the opposite side of the room.

"Serena, it's Nathan! Call out!"

"I'm in the office!" She moved closer to Armand.

He stepped into the room, his Beretta pushed out in front of him.

She motioned toward Jack with her chin as she moved to the desk and pressed two fingers against Armand's neck. "Check him."

Nathan did the same to Jack, then shook his head. "He's gone."

She took a breath, then clicked the pistol to safe. "Mayor is, too."

Nathan sheathed his weapon and glanced around the room. "What the hell happened here?"

She shook her head. "I don't know."

There was movement toward the front of the house. She turned toward the door in time to see Erica step through the foyer. She gasped as her hands covered her mouth. "Dad?"

93

Kyle pulled the latch on the metal pole and pushed the long, red swing arm open. The far end caught the locking mechanism with a clang.

He gave another look at the tire tracks in the dirt: they were fresh, definitely made within the last two or three hours. He couldn't tell how many cars there were, but there looked to be at least three different tread patterns.

For the sake of being stealthy, he left his Jeep behind and walked up the road toward the deserted ghost town.

After fifteen minutes, he reached the first structure, the sheriff's station, one of several filming locations that had been completed. It included two jail cells, an office, and a small armory.

He climbed the three steps and peered through the dirt- and grime-covered windows. He didn't notice any movement.

Directly across the street was the blacksmith's shop, another fully built set. One of the large barn-sized doors was missing, and the other was half open, hanging on by one hinge. He pulled a small flashlight from his pocket and peered into the darkness. The anvil that he used to play with as a kid was gone. Most of the iron chains that hung along the wall were also missing. And aside from a handful of rodent nests tucked into the corners, the open-plan building was empty.

He clicked off the flashlight and peered around the shop's corner into the alley. Surprisingly, he saw a few old wooden barrels - he would have expected those to have been gone long ago - and a horse watering trough that was falling apart.

The structure next door was the third of the six filming sets, the barbershop, which was comprised of only a single room with four barber chairs. The walls had once held mirrors, but someone broke them not long after the production company left.

Across the street, next to the sheriff's station, was the protagonist's house. It was a two-story home built in the Queen Anne style, with a wrap-around porch, slatted shutters, and poured-glass windows with ornate trimmings.

A few years ago, a storm had rolled through and dropped a tree through the roof, leaving only the kitchen and study, both on the first floor, intact.

Beside that was the town's general store, building five of the six sets, and behind him, next to the barber shop, was the saloon.

He moseyed over to that one, pushed the half-sized double doors open, and stepped inside, imagining himself, as he had many times before, as the town's sheriff, walking into a smoke-filled room filled with gamblers, cheats, and scoundrels as the piano player paused for an instant and all eyes turned toward him.

As his eyes adjusted to the dark, he could see the silhouette of a person seated in a chair in the middle of the room. There appeared to be a thin rope wrapped around her body, and her wrists were bound to the chair's arms.

"Kyle!"

"Lauren?" As he stepped toward her, he heard footsteps behind him.

Something came at him from the shadows and smacked into the side of his head.

94

Erica was sitting on the couch in the living room. From where she stood, just inside Armand's office, Serena couldn't hear what she and the two Highway Patrol officers were saying. But, she imagined, they weren't getting the whole truth, if any at all.

"Hey, Boss," Bob pulled her back from her thoughts.

She turned to face him. "Yeah."

"They found something." He motioned with his head toward the desk. "You need to see this."

She followed him through the office, where two detectives were sifting through the desk drawers. One of them was examining the contents of a large manila envelope. As she approached, she saw Kyle's name written on it with a black Sharpie. "What's that?"

The detective pulled a stack of one-hundred-dollar bills from the envelope. From the looks of it, several stacks, just like it, were still inside. He glanced up at her. "I was hoping maybe you could tell me. Isn't this the name of your previous sheriff?"

She nodded. "It is. But I've never seen that."

"We need to speak with him, all the same. Do you know where we can find him?"

She shook her head. "No, I haven't heard from him today. I've tried calling, but it goes to voicemail."

"Is that normal? Him ditching your calls?"

She frowned. "More often than you'd think, these days."

The coroner had removed the bodies almost an hour ago, and the investigators were still taking photos of the room. She moved closer to the table in the corner, where she found Jack. Blood soaked the chair and the carpet underneath.

Nathan stepped up behind her. "Boss, they're ready to cut Erica loose."

She turned to face him, then glanced at the detectives by the desk. She leaned in close and whispered, "Keep an eye on her. I want to know where she goes and what she does."

From the look on his face, she could tell that he was confused.

"Given that Kyle has gone off the grid again, I don't want to take any chances."

He nodded. "I'm on it."

"And if you see Bob, can you tell him I'm looking for him?"

"Will do."

"Thanks."

He turned, left the office, and returned to the living room.

She watched the exchange of words between him, the detectives, and Erica, who dabbed her eyes with a tissue as she rose from the couch.

She's quite the actress.

95

Kyle could hear someone calling his name as the world slowly came back into focus.

It was a familiar voice, one filled with concern.

"Kyle?" It said. "Oh, thank God! Kyle, wake up!"

He opened his eyes.

It was bright, and it was dusty. "Where am I?"

"We're in the old saloon." It was a female voice. It sounded like...

"Lauren?" His eyes focused on his surroundings. Someone had tied his hands behind him and bound his feet together. He couldn't move.

"I'm here," she answered.

He twisted his neck as far as he could and saw Lauren in a similar situation, on the far side of the room, next to the piano. "You okay?"

"I'm fine. Are you okay?"

"It's too early to tell. I can't feel my feet. How long was I out?"

"Maybe half an hour."

He pulled at the bindings, but the strings around his wrist didn't budge. "What happened?"

"What happened?" a male voice answered. "You poked your nose where it didn't belong."

The voice had a thick accent and came from behind him. He attempted - and failed - to turn far enough to see who it belonged to.

"Who are you?"

"That's none of your business, Sheriff. All you need to know is that this will all be over soon enough."

"What does that mean, 'It'll all be over?'"

"It means whatever you want it to mean. You get to decide your own outcome. Either you walk away a rich man, or you die here today.

Either way, as I said, it'll all be over."

He was about to say something else, but the sound of a car pulling to a stop out front caught his attention. He heard the engine shut off, then a door shut.

Erica walked in through the half-doors. She paused long enough to have a glance around the room.

"Sheriff. I knew that was your car back there. I'm surprised to see you here."

"As I am you. You mind telling me why I'm tied up like this?"

Her head tilted. "That's a good question." She looked past him. "Paolo, why is our guest tied up like that?"

The floorboards creaked behind him. "I didn't know what else to do with him."

She folded her arms across her chest. "Do you think you can behave if I let you out?"

Kyle nodded. "Of course."

She motioned to him with the wave of her hand. "Untie him."

96

Serena stepped out of the detective's way as he came up the sidewalk toward her, carrying what looked like a small briefcase. She gave a half-hearted smile as he passed. "I'm sorry, Nathan, you're breaking up. You're where?" She pressed the radio closer to her ear.

"I'm at the Old West town, on Chester Mountain. I followed her as far as I could. Had to park down a side road so she wouldn't see me."

"What's she doing up there?"

"I'm not sure. I'm coming up behind the barber shop now. I can see her car through the alley, so she's around here somewhere."

"Be careful. I'll get Bob, and we'll meet you there as soon as we can."

"Copy that, Boss. You want me to make contact when I find her?"

"Negative. Stay out of sight. I don't want you putting yourself in danger if you don't have to."

"Got it." He paused. "And Boss, Kyle's car is here, too."

She took a breath. "Of course it is." She glanced up in time to see Bob appear at the front door. She motioned for him to come over. "Thirty minutes. Stay safe."

"Copy that."

She clipped the radio to her belt and turned toward Bob.

"Hey, Boss. They're starting to pack up in there."

"How's Mary?"

"As well as can be, all things considered. Her sister should be here soon."

She nodded. "Beverly. Right. There's a conversation that I'm glad I won't be a part of."

He grinned.

"Nathan followed Erica up to the Old West town. He lost her when he had to park out of the way, then he found her car outside the barber shop."

"What's she doing up there?"

"That's what we're going to find out. Give Betty a call, let her know where we're going, and then meet me up there as soon as you can. We'll meet up at the fire access road and find our way to Nathan."

He nodded, then turned toward the driveway. He stopped after two steps and turned back. "Hey, have you heard from Kyle? I tried calling, but I got his answering machine."

"No, but we can talk to him when we get there. Nathan found his Jeep parked outside the gate."

"What the hell is he doing up there?"

She shrugged. "How about we go find out?"

He nodded, then continued to his patrol car.

97

Erica sat across the table from Kyle. "Is there anything I can get you, Sheriff?"

He glanced across the room to where Lauren was still tied to the chair. Paolo had shoved an old rag into her mouth when she started screaming at him.

"You can untie her. And get that damned thing out of her mouth."

She shook her head. "I'm afraid that's one thing I can't do."

"Why not? You can't possibly consider her a threat."

"I think we'll leave her as she is, for now. I'm not her favorite person at the moment."

"Why's that?"

"Because I have her daughter."

His eyes grew wide, and he jumped out of the chair so quickly that it slid a few feet across the floor. "You what?"

Paolo was leaning against the bar on the far side of the room. He stood and took a step toward them.

She held her hand up, stopping him. "Calm down, Sheriff. She's fine. She's with an associate of mine. As long as you do everything I say, I'll return her precious little girl, no harm done."

"As long as I… what exactly do you expect me to do?"

"For starters, have a seat and take a deep breath."

He stared down at her but didn't move.

She didn't want to use threats, but she was prepared to do so if it came to that. She lifted the pistol from her lap and set it on the table, the barrel facing him. "I said have a seat."

His eyes briefly dropped to the gun, then he re-met her gaze.

"Don't make me beg," she said.

He retrieved the chair, pulled it closer to the table, and lowered himself into it. "Where's Molly?"

"I told you. She's safe."

"Where?"

"Look, sheriff, we can go back and forth like this all day. I really don't care. But the thing is, the girl... Molly, you said her name was?"

He nodded.

"Well, you see, Molly is about an hour away from being thrown into the trunk of a car and driven down to Florida. Once there, she'll be crammed into a shipping container with about seventy-five to a hundred other girls around her age. The next time she sees daylight, she'll be in another country. After that... who knows?"

By the look on his face, she knew he didn't like what she was saying.

"What do you want?"

She chuckled. "You're the third person today who asked me that question."

He didn't seem amused.

"Okay. Here's what I want." She leaned toward him. "I want you to go to the state police and turn yourself in. Tell them you were in the room when Jack and my dad shot each other."

"I'm sorry, what?"

"Shhh... don't interrupt. Tell them they started arguing when your dear mayor gave you your cut of the business, and Jack was upset because you were getting paid more than he was."

"What the hell are you talking about?"

"I said, don't interrupt." She thumbed the hammer of the pistol. "Tell them that you've been working with the mayor ever since your dad was killed."

"Who ever said my dad was killed?"

"Oops." She shrugged. "You got me."

98

Serena heard a vehicle coming up the road behind her. She closed the trunk of her rental car and turned, expecting to see Bob's patrol car. Instead, a black four-door Chevy Suburban pulled to a stop a few feet away.

The driver's and rear passenger's doors opened simultaneously. A rather large African American man in a skin-tight t-shirt and blue jeans stepped down from the front, and a very well-dressed man in an expensive-looking suit climbed out from the back.

"I'm sorry, folks, this area is closed."

The man in the suit began walking toward her while the other disappeared behind the truck.

"Don't worry, miss. We mean you no harm."

"Who are you?"

"I'm here for Kyle. We're old friends. Go way back."

She peered around him, attempting to see where the other man went. "You got a name, old friend of Kyles?"

He held his hand out as he slowly approached. "You can call me Tony."

She took his hand. "Tony." It took a second before recognition set in. "Tony Lombardi?"

Tony smiled. "I see my reputation precedes me. And you must be Serena."

How does he…?

"Kyle speaks very highly of you."

"Does he?"

He nodded. "He does." The other man came up behind him. "Allow me to introduce my associate, Junior."

As Junior stepped around Tony, she noticed he was holding a shotgun in one hand and a hunting rifle in the other. He handed the rifle to Tony, then stretched his now empty hand toward her. "Pleased to meet you, ma'am."

She shook his hand. "What are you planning to do with those? It's a little late in the season for hunting."

Tony smiled. "As I said, I'm here for Kyle."

She frowned. "Do you know something I don't?"

"There's no doubt about that, bambolotta, but I won't bore you with my vast array of knowledge."

Junior pulled his arm back. "What's the plan, Boss?"

Tony turned to his companion. "Are we sure they're in the saloon?"

Junior nodded. "Marco has eyes on him as we speak."

"He's unharmed?"

He nodded.

"Then let's keep it that way. You meet up with Marco and find out where everyone else is. I'll go in through the front and give her the chance to surrender."

Serena held her hand up. "Hang on a second."

Tony lifted his index finger and continued. "If you see that weasel Pay-olo, don't hesitate. I want him dead."

Junior nodded. "Got it." He turned and vanished into the woods.

"You're not going to kill anyone," Serena said.

"It won't be the first time. And believe me, that bastard deserves much worse."

"That's not for you to decide."

"Maybe not. But that's never stopped me before."

"Are you confessing to killing someone?"

"I'm not confessing anything. Just stating a fact."

"You know I'm the sheriff, right?"

He sighed as he looked her up and down. "I won't hold that against you."

99

Shadows played along the walls as the sunlight gave way to the night.

Erica had moved them to a room on the second floor for 'privacy,' and Kyle was pacing in front of a broken window next to an old wooden bed frame.

"What's your answer, Sheriff?"

He turned to face her. "You know I'm not the sheriff, right? I was relieved of my duties last week."

"I know. But it sounds better than 'Kyle.' Frankly, I never liked that name. I rank it up there with Seth. Seth is a stupid name, too."

He frowned. "Do we really want to waste time talking about names?"

She shrugged. "Doesn't matter to me." She glanced down at the small silver watch on her wrist. "In about thirty minutes, when we hit that deadline, I'll be fifty thousand dollars richer. So, take all the time you need. Of course, if you decline my offer, I turn you over to Paolo, and, well, your time will be up. So to speak."

"So, my options are to turn myself in to the police and confess to crimes I had no part in, to save Molly, or die?"

She nodded. "Yeah. Sounds simple, doesn't it?"

"Okay."

"Okay?"

"Okay."

She rose from the chair. "Okay, what?"

"I'll turn myself in."

Erica smiled. "I thought you'd see things my way."

"But first, you need to tell me what you meant when you said, 'got me.'"

"Sorry?"

"Downstairs, when you said that my dad was killed. As far as everyone knows, he had a heart attack."

She smiled. "Which is true. But he did have a little help."

"Armand?"

"Are you kidding? Dad doesn't have the stones to do something like that." She chuckled. "I slipped something into his drink earlier in the day. It took longer than I expected, but it got the job done." She grinned. "You want to kill me, don't you?"

"Honestly, yes. But I'll settle to see you stand trial for his murder."

"Do you really think that'll happen? After all we've been through? Don't forget that I saved all those poor children. I'm a hero."

"Anonymous hero. You wanted to stay out of the spotlight, remember?"

"Yeah, well, things can change. Especially after your confession and the investigation that'll be sure to follow."

She turned to the door and pulled it open. The henges squealed. "Paolo, call Reuben. Tell him to bring the girl." She turned back and motioned to the open door. "Shall we?"

He crossed the room and went through the door. Because of the building's open floor plan, he saw that Paolo was lying on the floor, his head resting in a small puddle of red liquid.

Erica pushed him aside and leaned over the railing. "What the hell?" She ran past him to the stairs and started down them.

A gunshot stopped her dead in her tracks. She ducked into the nearest room and slammed the door behind her.

Kyle found cover behind an old whiskey barrel, knowing that the frail wood wouldn't stop a slingshot, let alone a bullet.

"Kyle, you okay?"

He peered around the barrel. "Tony? Is that you?"

"In the flesh! Are you hurt?"

"No, I'm good."

"Thank God! I didn't realize you were up there. I saw that bitch, and my trigger finger just went crazy!"

"There was a woman down there…"

"She's safe. I got her out and told her where to find your cop friend." Tony climbed the steps and offered him a pistol.

"Thanks for the rescue."

"Uh-huh. She go in there?"

Kyle nodded. "On three?"

"Fuck that." Tony shoved his shoulder into the door, and it splintered off the hinges. He rushed into the room, his rifle at the ready.

Kyle followed him through.

All they saw of Erica was her leg as it disappeared through the window. Tony brought his rifle to bear.

Kyle reached out and smacked it away.

"The fuck you do that for?"

"I need her alive! She kidnapped that woman's child, and she confessed to killing my dad!"

"Well fuck. Guess we better go after her, then."

100

Erica chanced a look over her shoulder as she ducked into the alley, almost tripping over a wooden bucket. A few feet away, she saw three large barrels grouped together. She dropped behind them and rested her back against the wall.

She could feel the adrenaline running through her, and she was pretty sure her ankle gave way when she hit the ground, but it wasn't hurting.

Yet.

Jesus Christ, that was close! Was that Tony? It looked like Tony. How the hell did he find me? And what the fuck is he doing here?

She cautiously peered around the barrel and listened. No one was following her.

There's no way they're not looking for me.

She glanced to her left. Just outside the alley, maybe fifty feet away, the national forest offered a safe refuge.

Think, Erica. How are you going to get out of this one?

The car was parked out in the open, and Tony would surely have someone watching it, so that wasn't an option.

The forest? If I can make it to the road… then what? The nearest town is fifteen miles away, at least. That's way too far.

Maybe if I avoid the main roads and stick to the secondaries…

She heard voices. They were looking for her.

She shot another look at the trees.

That old train station isn't too far. I can hide there and wait until night. Then I can reassess, regroup, and come up with a plan.

"She's back here!"

She turned to see Junior jogging in her direction. She'd never seen

223

him run, and if the current situation wasn't so serious, she might have found it humorous.

She pushed herself away from the wall and ran full tilt toward the trees.

A shotgun blast destroyed the barrel she'd just used as cover, sending wood shards flying in all directions. She reached out behind her and fired a blind shot back at him.

She heard him yell, "Fuck!"

Must have hit him.

She didn't risk stopping or turning to verify that suspicion.

The trees were getting closer.

"She's running into the woods!"

That wasn't Junior, and it wasn't Tony or Kyle. That was an unfamiliar voice, and it came from above her.

Do they have people on the roof, too?

A bullet slammed into a tree inches from her shoulder as the forest welcomed her into their embrace. She kept running, changing her direction whenever she came upon an obstacle too big to jump over or too low to duck under.

Train station it is!

101

It was dark, and even though Erica's eyes had adjusted to the night, it was still difficult for her to see anything. The sky was overcast, blocking out the waning gibbous moon. Every now and then, it would peek through, giving her hope, but it never stayed out for longer than a few seconds.

How long have I been walking? Am I even going in the right direction? Jesus, my ankle hurts.

The adrenaline had worn off... she didn't know how long ago, and the shoe on her left foot felt like it was getting tighter. She hadn't even realized that she'd started limping until five minutes ago when she had to step over a small fallen tree.

She stopped and leaned against the trunk of a large red maple. Even in the dark, she could see the beauty of the red leaves above.

She focused on her breathing, trying to ignore her throbbing ankle. She knew that it was swollen and possibly sprained or worse, and she wanted to look, but she was certain that if she took her shoe off, it wouldn't go back on.

There was laughter from somewhere nearby. She peered through the trees and turned in all directions, trying to find the source. Finally, she zeroed in on where she thought it had come from and limped toward it.

A few feet away, the trees opened up, and the once majestic, fake train station revealed itself.

The fading blue and white paint was chipping in most places, and rotting wood poked through in others. Surprisingly, despite being the main hangout for teens from the surrounding counties, who were not known for respecting state property, a handful of the windows had survived.

The grass-overgrown train rails ran alongside the front for about two hundred feet in either direction. Being a filming set, there was no need to go any farther than that. She knew that the passenger car that was used in the pilot episode rested somewhere on the other side, behind the building.

The one feature that stood out the most, however, was the fire burning in an old steel barrel on the front landing. A small group of teens was nearby, drinking, laughing, and dancing to some godawful noise blasting from a portable stereo system.

She slid the gun into her front pocket and hobbled up to the door. The small crowd didn't even seem to notice as she limped past and entered the darkness of the lobby.

102

Sunday, September 30, 1990

Kyle took the bottle from Serena and unscrewed the top. He swirled the water, watching the mini tornado in the plastic container before taking a sip. "Thank you."

She nodded. "It's not coffee, but it's all I got."

"It's fine. Thanks." He handed her the bottle. "Are we ready?"

She nodded. "I'm ready."

Next to her, Bob and Nathan confirmed that they, too, were ready.

"Let's do this," Bob said.

Kyle grasped the slide of his Beretta and gently pulled it rearward to verify that a round was chambered. "Remember, we need her alive. She has Molly somewhere, and we need to find her."

They all nodded in agreement.

Nathan swung the sling of his rifle over his shoulder and adjusted it. "We sure she's even in there?"

Kyle shook his head. "Not for certain, no. But we may get lucky. Junior said she was limping. She couldn't have gone far."

Bob glanced down at his watch. "How long ago was that?"

"It was last night. Around what, eight? Eight thirty?"

"Something like that," Serena offered.

Bob unholstered his pistol and glanced up at the train station. They had all parked out of sight and walked the rest of the way. If Erica was inside, they didn't want her to know they were coming. "That was ten hours ago, at least. If she did stop here, there's a good chance she's not here now."

"I know," Kyle said. He looked back at the structure, carefully examining every window and every door. "Let's go."

227

Without another word, they moved to surround the building, sticking to the trees for cover as much as possible. Nathan went right, Serena left, and Bob made his way to the rear.

They all held short of the clearing, keeping a direct line of sight to each other.

Kyle waited until the others gave him a thumbs-up before flashing his own. He held his hand up, fingers spread.

His thumb folded down.

The others mimicked him.

His index finger tucked underneath his thumb.

The others mimicked him.

He continued the countdown until all fingers were folded, and then he hurriedly made his way to the front door. Out of his periphery, he saw Serena and the two deputies move in on their respective sides.

When he reached the front door, he pressed his side against the wall, dropped onto his left knee, and slowly peered around the corner.

The morning light was streaming through the windows to his right, where Nathan would breach, but everything on his left was dark.

That's where Serena would be coming in.

The ticketing booth was in the center of the room, blocking his view of the rear wall. He'd have to wait for the signal from the other two when Bob was ready.

103

Erica sat in the sand, her arms wrapped around her legs. The water rushed in, just high enough to cover her feet, which sank into the sand as it receded back into the ocean.

She closed her eyes and tilted her head back, feeling the warmth of the sun on her face, and smiled.

Behind her, a man's voice called out. "Erica!"

She turned, attempting to see who it was. She thought she was alone and had the beach to herself.

"Erica, you in here?"

The world around her shifted, and she felt like she was being pulled away.

"Nathan, anything?"

That was a female voice. It sounded familiar.

"Nothing yet, Boss"

A third voice? How many were there?

She sat up, instantly realizing that she'd been dreaming.

She was surrounded by darkness. Her ankle was screaming at her.

She grabbed the pistol off the floor and slid up against the wall behind her.

A shadow blocked out the tiny streak of light that was filtering through the floorboards above, and dirt fell toward her. She squinted and waited for it to clear.

"Check the ticket booth."

Fuck. That's Kyle.

"On it."

And that's the sheriff... Serena. The other one must be the deputy.

"I'll head back outside and check the perimeter."

And there's the other one. That's all four. Is Tony up there, too?

She thumbed the safety to the off position and stood, pushing against the wall for support and keeping as much weight off her ankle as possible.

She was in a closet in the basement. It seemed like the safest place to take a nap.

How long was I out?

She checked her watch.

Ten hours? Shit!

She had hoped to be on her way to Florida by now.

She was trapped down here, with nowhere to go if they found her. She needed to find a way out of the building.

She pressed the magazine release and counted eight rounds. With one in the chamber, that gave her... not nearly enough to last a prolonged gunfight.

Fuck.

"She's not here, Boss," the deputy with the deep voice said. "I'll check outside with Bob."

"Ticket booth's clear."

Serena.

"Damn. I knew it was a long shot. Alright, let's make sure she's not outside somewhere, then head back to town."

Kyle.

Two sets of footsteps crossed the room above, headed away from her.

She closed her eyes and sighed.

Thank you, Jesus.

"Hang on," Kyle said. "Isn't there a basement?"

Fuck!

104

Serena nodded. "I think there is. Do you remember where the stairs are?" She searched the area in the darkness, looking for a way to get downstairs.

"No, I've never been down there. I remember hearing the kids at school talk about it."

She pulled her flashlight from her pocket and swept the room. "There's a door over there."

"I've got one over here, too."

She crossed to the door and pulled it open. "Found it."

She saw Kyle pull his door open. "Here, too. These go up."

"You go up, I go down?"

He shone his light up the stairs, then looked back at her. "Be careful."

"You too." She held her Beretta out in front, resting her wrist on her other hand, allowing her to move the weapon and light simultaneously, and descended the stairs.

As she neared the bottom, she realized the basement stretched farther than she'd expected. There were several doors on the far side to her left and a short hall on her right, with even more doors, six in all, three toward the rear of the building, three toward the front.

A rat ran across the floor in front of her, taking her off guard. "Mierda!" She took a breath. "Odio las ratas!"

The basement was cold and damp. She wondered how many types of molds she might be breathing in as she left the hallway behind and made her way to the doors on the far side.

Something, somewhere, creaked.

The building settling?

It's an old structure. Shouldn't it have settled by now?

She grabbed the handle of one door and slowly pulled it open enough to shine her light into the room.

The door flung open, taking her by surprise, and banged into her hand. The flashlight fell to the ground and slid across the floor.

Someone grabbed her gun, and she felt a body slam into her. She tightened her grip on the weapon as Erica tried to rip it from her grasp.

She flung her elbow up to strike back.

Erica ducked out of the way and then rammed the top of her head against her chin. Serena felt her teeth crunch together, and she stumbled backward, disoriented.

The two rapid-fired gunshots were deafening in the closed space. She felt like she had just been hit in the chest by a bodybuilder with a baseball bat.

She couldn't breathe. The darkness of the basement seemed to get darker as she fell backward.

105

Erica tucked the sheriff's Beretta into her waistband and stood.

This wasn't my plan.

Footsteps pounded on the floor above.

"Serena!" Kyle yelled. "Serena, call out!"

Ignoring the pain as best she could, she hobbled toward the stairs.

The footsteps above paused a few feet from the door at the top of the stairwell. "Nathan! Bob! On me!"

She took the chance and hurried to the hallway on the other side, pulled the nearest door open, and stepped inside. She closed the door, leaving enough room to watch the stairs.

The three men descended, flashlights lighting up the area below them.

Kyle swung his light to his left. "Serena!"

He sprinted toward her, the other two deputies close behind.

Now or never.

She hobbled up the stairs. By the time she reached the top step, she couldn't ignore her ankle anymore. As she made her way to the nearest exit, her foot dragged behind her.

She was aware of her uninjured foot thumping on the floor, no doubt alerting her pursuers below. She grabbed the edge of the partially open door.

"Erica!"

She instinctively fired a shot behind her as she rushed into the crisp morning air.

Bullets ripped through the door behind her, and she dove to the ground. She rolled onto her back and returned fire. Three shots, four, five, she lost count.

The slide of her pistol locked open. The magazine was empty. She tossed it aside, grabbed Serena's Beretta from her belt, and held it toward the door as she rose to her feet and stumbled down the steps and into the grass. Her ankle gave out, and she fell. She kept the pistol aimed at the door while she gathered herself.

Come on, Kyle. Show your face.

The door slowly creaked open. She pulled the trigger and fired two rounds through it.

She waited.

Did I get him? Is he dead?

Even if you did, there are still two more. You need to run!

She rolled onto her side, pushed herself up, and sprinted toward the tree line. Her ankle rolled every few steps.

"Erica!"

He's not dead.

Keep running.

Ankle is killing me!

Ignore it! Keep going!

A shot rang out, and a chunk of bark flew off the tree beside her. She shielded her face with her arm.

The ground suddenly gave out, and she tumbled down a steep hill. It felt like forever until she finally stopped.

Fuck. I think I broke my leg.

At least I still have the gun.

She traced the path she'd fallen to the top of the hill. The outline of a man caught her attention, but she couldn't tell who it was. She scooted aside and leaned her back against a tree.

106

Kyle looked over the edge, attempting to see where she went, his pistol at the ready. All he saw were trees.

"Kyle, come in." It was Bob.

He keyed the mic on his radio. "Go ahead."

"Anything?"

"No, she got away."

"But it was her?"

"Yeah." He took a breath. "It was her. How's Serena?"

"She's in a lot of pain, but she's alive. She'll have one hell of a bruise."

No doubt.

"What's the plan?" Bob asked.

"I'm gonna track her. Have Nathan get Serena to the hospital. Then grab your car and meet me at the fire road to the west. I'll chase her your way. Be ready when we get there."

"Copy that, Boss."

I'm not the boss.

He grabbed a low-hanging branch on the tree nearest him and began the arduous journey to the bottom.

After a few slips and several scratches on his arms, he made it to his destination.

Flattened leaves and small, broken branches and twigs were scattered all around the spot where she had landed.

He kneeled, examining a spot where she might have pushed herself upright. To him, it looked like she was dragging something behind her.

Is her leg broken? Her ankle? Either way, she can't have gone far. Should be easy enough to follow her.

The trail she left behind led to the west, right toward the fire road. As long as Bob gets there before she does, she should be in handcuffs before breakfast.

A few feet further, he saw a small hole in the ground, and the drag marks were gone.

Is that a makeshift cane? Clever. She can move a little faster, but still not fast enough.

I hope.

He continued on, watching the ground, watching the trees. One thing he didn't see was blood. So, any injuries she had were internal.

"That's far enough, Sheriff!" It was Erica.

He crouched, scanning the forest. He didn't see her. "I'm not..."

"... not the sheriff. I know. Do you know how grating that is? You really should come up with some new material."

"And yet, you still call me that."

"Old habits."

He caught movement to his right and focused in that direction. "You're hurt. You're not gonna get very far. Why don't you turn yourself in?"

"Sorry, Sheriff. There's too many things I want to do, and being in jail isn't one of them."

Now it sounded like the voice came from behind him, and he aimed his pistol in that direction. "Plans like taking over your dad's drug smuggling business?"

"That and more."

"You mean kidnapping little kids and selling them into slavery?"

"You think you know what you're talking about, but you don't."

"Where's Molly?" He kept trying to nail down where she was.

"Molly? Who's... Oh, right. The girl. She's probably in Florida."

"Where? Who has her?"

"Like I'm gonna tell you that. Come on, Kyle."

"I had to try."

There was a long silence.

"Erica?"

She didn't answer.

"Erica. You still with me?"

Birds were waking up, singing their morning songs.

Otherwise, Kyle felt like he was the only person out there.

107

Serena was sitting in the passenger seat of Nathan's patrol car. "I'm fine!" Her breathing was labored, and her chest hurt.

"Of course you are. You're a tough gal. But you were shot at point-blank range, and you're going to the hospital to get checked out."

"I'm your boss, Deputy. You don't give me orders!"

"I'm fully aware of that. But the fact remains. You're going to the hospital."

She glared at him. "You're fired. Now get out of my way." She tried to stand.

He held his hand up, blocking her from getting out of the car. "While I appreciate the kind gesture, I don't accept. Now sit down. Please."

Is he serious?

"Getting fired isn't something you can't not accept. You're no longer a deputy. Now move out of my way, or I'll arrest you for obstruction."

He tapped his finger against her ballistic vest. Her chest felt like it was on fire, and she lost her breath. She fell back into the seat. "Yeah, you have a broken rib. Maybe two. No more arguing. Get in."

She swung her legs inside the car.

"Don't worry about the seatbelt. It'll hurt like hell. I'll drive gently."

She gave the best smile she could. "Already hurts like hell."

Nathan closed the door and rounded the front of the car.

Up the road, she saw a black Suburban coming toward them.

What the hell? What is he doing here?

Nathan saw it, too, and he went to intercept the truck. The rear passenger window went down, and Tony popped his head out. After a quick exchange of words that she couldn't hear due to being so far away, Tony's door opened. He got out, and he and Nathan came back to the car.

Nathan opened her door.

"Sheriff," Tony said. "Jesus. You okay?"

"I've been better."

"Your deputy told me you were shot, but it looks worse than he let on."

She weakly smiled. "Thanks. Just what every girl wants to hear."

"I'm gonna send Junior to the hospital with you. Your deputy's gonna come with me, and we're gonna go find Kyle."

"No need. Thanks, though."

"No, really. He got a splinter in his face when Erica shot at him. He's done nothing but complain all night. I can't take any more of his whining."

A gunshot rang out. Nathan and Tony turned toward the direction it came from, and Junior jumped out of the Suburban, shotgun in hand.

108

Kyle was angry.

Angry at Armand Hawthorne for starting all of this.

Angry at his father for leaving him to clean it up.

Angry at Jack for killing his coworker, his friend.

Angry at Erica for kidnapping Lauren's daughter.

But mostly, right then, he was most angry at himself.

His pistol was still pointed at her, a tiny wisp of smoke wafting skyward, the after-effects of a controlled explosion of a nine-millimeter projectile leaving the stainless-steel barrel, mixed with the cold, crisp morning air.

Erica was dead. Of that, he was certain. And with her, any hope of finding Molly.

Keeping his weapon trained on his target, he kneeled and picked up Serena's stolen service weapon.

"God dammit, Erica. I told you not to do that."

After he tucked the Beretta into his belt at the small of his back, he used his now free hand to feel her neck for a pulse. There was none.

He sighed and holstered his pistol. "Fuck."

He fell backward, sat on the damp ground, and rubbed his eyes. "Fuck."

He raised his face toward the rising sun and took a deep breath. "FUCK!"

The dense forest seemed to absorb his words and answered with silence.

A faint beep emanated from somewhere on the lifeless body.

He pushed himself to his knees and searched Erica's front pockets. They were empty. He rolled her onto her side and found a Motorola pager in her back pocket.

It beeped again and vibrated as a number flashed on the tiny screen: 911.

He pressed the left arrow and scrolled through the incoming numbers. He didn't recognize most of them, but there was one that had called several times over the past few days. That one, he knew.

He knew it because he'd called that number countless times over the years.

Beverly.

How is she involved in all of this? I know she was in a relationship with Armand.

Armand was working with Tony.

And then there's that whole kidnapping mess that he was into, that Erica was into.

Did she know what Armand was doing?

How could she not?

And what about Erica? Why would Beverly be contacting her?

He could feel a headache coming on as he closed his eyes and fell back onto the ground. He kicked his legs out as his arms dropped to his sides.

He stared past the treetops to the pink clouds high above.

"Fuck."

109

The sun was high as Kyle stood on the porch of Beverly's Inn, gazing out across the recently plowed wheat field. A few miles beyond that, the trees on Chester Mountain were losing their leaves.

To his right, Nathan and Bob both clicked the safety off on their rifles. He turned and glanced back at the Tennessee Highway Patrol SWAT team sprinting toward them across the driveway, leaving their armored van behind. He closed his eyes and took a deep breath, preparing for what came next.

The team reached the porch, and the lead officer tapped his shoulder. He ducked back to the end of the line, giving way to the four highly trained officers.

Three seconds later, a hand-held battering ram shattered the wood surrounding the doorknob, and the three deputies followed the SWAT officers into the quaint bed-and-breakfast.

Nathan followed two of them to the left and into the dining room. The other two went straight down the hallway into the kitchen, and Kyle led Bob up the stairs.

Once they hit the landing, Kyle swung right and swept the room with the stylized "A," while Bob did the same with "B."

"Clear," Kyle said.

"Clear," Bob answered.

Kyle turned and followed him to the bathroom. Bob grasped the glass doorknob and then looked back at Kyle, who nodded. Bob twisted the knob, and the door swung open. Kyle stepped in and swept the tiny room. "Clear."

Bob lowered his rifle and met Kyles' gaze.

Downstairs, they heard similar callouts from various voices:

"Kitchen clear," "Dining room clear," "Bedroom clear," "Bathroom clear."

There was a pause. "House is clear!"

Kyle clicked his rifle to safe and frowned. "Dammit." He motioned for Bob to head down the stairs.

"I've got something." It was one of the SWAT team members.

"What is it?" Another officer asked.

"Looks like a secret door."

Kyle and Bob found Nathan outside the main bedroom, his weapon in the low-ready position, and fell in behind him.

"Closet," Nathan said.

Kyle peered around him into the room. The SWAT team looked like they were entering a portal into another dimension: the doors of a wardrobe were wide open, and they were stepping through what he imagined had to be a hole in the back.

Once the last team member passed through, Kyle inched closer, where he saw that the back of the wardrobe was missing, and the team was descending a hidden staircase.

110

Serena stepped into the diner and looked around.

Even without the vest underneath her uniform shirt, it still hurt like hell to breathe.

"Are you up for this?" Kyle asked as Nathan and Bob came in behind him.

She nodded. "I'm fine."

"You sure? We can…"

"I said I'm fine."

He gave her a worried look.

"I need to see this through."

He nodded.

Ethel came up beside them. "Can I get you a seat, Sheriff?"

She shook her head. "No, thank you. We're looking for someone."

"Well, if you tell me who it is, I can tell you if they're here or not."

"Thanks. We'll have a look ourselves."

She frowned, then left.

"Well, if it ain't my favorite sheriff and his deputy!" Otis called out from a nearby booth. He swiveled his wheelchair around to face them.

Bob grinned and rushed to his side. He reached his hand out, and Otis took it. "It's nice to see you back on your feet, Otis!"

"In a manner of speakin'. Thanks." His head tilted, and he smiled up at Serena. "Ladies and gentlemen!" He called out. "A round of applause for the men… and woman… of Millhaven's finest! Without them, I surely wouldn't be alive today!"

Everyone in the diner, patrons and staff alike, began clapping. A few of them whistled.

She held her hands up, palms out. "Okay, okay. That's enough.

Thank you." She smiled at Otis. "You know we were just doing our jobs, right?"

"Hm. So you say. But you and me, we both know you'd be sad if I wasn't around."

She grinned and shot him a wink. "Don't tell anyone."

"Boss," Nathan said.

She turned and followed his gaze, and she saw Bea, Dorthea, and Beverly seated at a table near the back wall. She started toward them.

Kyle and the two deputies followed.

When they reached the table, the three women looked up.

"Good morning, Sheriff," Bea said.

"Bea," Serena nodded at her. "Dorthea. I hope you ladies are having a pleasant afternoon."

Dorthea set her napkin on the table and smiled. "We certainly are. What brings the entire sheriff's department here?"

"Not that we mind, of course." Bea was shifting her gaze between all three men.

Serena wasn't exactly sure, but she thought Bea might have been checking her out, too. "We need to speak with Beverly."

Beverly coughed into her water glass as she took a sip.

"Beverly?" Bea asked.

"Does this have anything to do with her affair with the mayor?" Dorthea asked.

Every diner within earshot turned toward them, their faces covered with expressions that ranged from shock to humor to confirmation.

Beverly set her glass down. "I'm not sure what we might have to talk about."

Kyle stepped forward. "Do you want to follow us outside, or should we do this here?"

She looked at him disapprovingly. "Don't you take that tone with me. I practically raised you!"

Serena nodded. "Right. We'll do it here, then." She pulled a set of handcuffs from the pouch on her belt. "Beverly Woodson, you're under arrest for kidnapping, illegal transportation of minors across state lines, harboring a fugitive, aiding and abetting, and trafficking in illicit narcotics."

"This is ridiculous!"

"Stand up."

She didn't move.

Nathan rounded the table and grabbed one of her arms. Bob

grabbed the other. Together, they pulled her from the chair.

By now, they had the full attention of everyone in the diner.

"I was only doing what Armand told me to do! He was the mastermind behind everything!"

Kyle stepped aside as the two deputies guided Beverly toward the exit.

"Save it," Serena said. "We know you and Erica were working together."

"How could you possibly…?"

"We found your safe. We found your records. We have the names of every child you abducted and where they went."

There were quite a few gasps throughout the diner.

"You have the right to remain silent," she continued.

111

Friday, November 9, 1990 - 2 Months later

Kyle gently set the black duffel bag onto the red velvet-lined pool table between the white cue ball and Tony's stick.

"You got a death wish? I sink this, I win Junior's money."

"Yeah? How much?"

Tony glanced behind him, and Kyle saw Junior leaning against the wall. "How much was the bet?"

Junior shrugged. "I forget. Ten bucks?"

Tony looked back at Kyle. "Ten bucks."

"Damn. You sure you can afford that?"

"Don't be a smart ass." He nodded at the bag. "What's that?"

"That is what I promised you for helping me."

"No shit?" He waved Junior over. "Open it." He glanced back at Kyle. "Not that I don't trust you. I just, you know, don't trust you."

"I take no offense."

Junior pulled the zipper open. "It looks like it's all there," he said.

"No shit?"

Junior nodded, then removed some of the cellophane-wrapped white bricks from the bag and placed them on the pool table.

"As promised," Kyle said.

"I'll be damned. How'd you pull this off?"

"It's probably better if you don't know." He took a breath. "We still have a deal? You keep this stuff out of Millhaven?"

Tony nodded. "We do, indeed. And thank you, Kyle."

He turned to leave. "I guess we're done then."

"So, what's next for the former sheriff of Podunk, Tennessee?"

He turned back. "What do you mean?"

"Well, you can't go back to being the sheriff. That fine little Bella Donna is doing that. How is she, by the way? She ever talk about me?"

He smiled. "She's fine."

"And then some."

"Anyway, to answer your question, I don't know what's next. I put my dad's house up for sale, and I'm just gonna take a month or two to travel. Try to figure out a few things."

"What about that girlfriend of yours? She going with you?"

"Girlfriend?"

"The one with the kid."

"Lauren. No. After all that happened, she moved to Maine to be closer to her parents. She said Millhaven wasn't a safe place anymore."

Tony nodded. His face turned serious. "I'm sorry to hear that. You know, your old man did right by me. You did right by me. If you ever need anything, you only need to ask."

"Thank you, Mr. Lombardi. I appreciate that."

"It's Tony. And think nothing of it."

Kyle nodded. "Same here."

Tony motioned to the bag, and Junior began repacking the bricks.

"Stay out of trouble, Tony."

"There's no danger of that ever happening."

112

It was Friday night, and Serena was on duty.

I really need to get a life.

She was leaning against the fender of the brand-new Ford Bronco Police truck, staring at the sky and attempting to piece the stars together into constellations.

She was never very good at astronomy.

Movement to her left caught her eye, and she turned to see a Buck step out of the trees and into the street. It was a ways away, but she thought she could see at least six points on his head.

"Hello, there."

He appeared to have heard her because he froze and looked in her direction. She didn't move.

You're okay. I'm no threat.

His head jerked to the right, and his body tensed up as if it were going to…

He bolted across the street, jumped over the guardrail, and vanished into the night as a car screeched around the bend and sped past.

She pulled the Bronco's door open, jumped into the driver's seat, and flipped a switch on the center console.

The red and blue roof lights came to life, and the siren screamed as she pulled the gear shifter into drive. Gravel flew up behind the truck, and the wheels screeched when they found the pavement.

The speeding car's headlights were off, and it was swerving from side to side.

Are they drunk?

She glanced down at the speedometer; they were quickly approaching fifty miles per hour.

I hope they know about that sharp curve up there.

Brake lights lit up the darkness in front of her, and the distance between the car and her Bronco closed rapidly. She swerved left to avoid running into the back of it as the car came to a stop in the middle of the road.

She shifted the truck into park, threw open the door, then rushed to the car.

The driver's window went down. "Hi, Sh-sh-sheriff. Beautiful night, huh?"

"Arnie? What the hell are you doing?"

He smiled at her, and she saw that one of his front teeth was missing. Judging by the swollen gums and dried blood on his mouth and chin, it had happened recently.

"Whose car is this?"

He shrugged. "D-d-don't know. I f-f-found it."

"You found it?"

Something banged loudly toward the rear of the car, and a muffled voice called out. She couldn't understand what it was saying.

She pointed to the trunk. "Is that Wes back there?"

He grinned.

Afterward

What you're holding is the culmination of over a year's work. What started out as "Hey, I'm going to write a story" turned into a 250-plus page manuscript. I shared my work with family and friends along the way, and at one point, I decided to release it into the wild. Hopefully, you'll enjoy reading this wild and unpredictable ride as much as I did writing it.

Thank you for your support. I truly appreciate each and every one of you.

Author Bio

Will Beaudry grew up reading Science Fiction and mystery novels. His favorite authors are Ian Fleming, Robert B. Parker, and Tom Clancy.

He fell in love with storytelling in grade school while taking a creative writing class and has been writing short stories, poems, and songs ever since.

Born into a family with strong military roots, Will enlisted in the U.S. Coast Guard right out of High School, where he was stationed in Portland, Maine. Later in life, he re-enlisted in the Army National Guard, where he was assigned to a Public Affairs Detachment, which afforded him the opportunity to hone his writing skills as a journalist.

He currently lives in Virginia with his wife, who shares his love of the outdoors. He is the lead instructor for a private security company, where he passes along his decades of knowledge in First Aid, Active Shooter Response, and fundamental law as mandated by the Virginia Department of Criminal Justice Services.

www.ingramcontent.com/pod-product-compliance
Lightning Source LLC
Chambersburg PA
CBHW050111280326
41933CB00010B/1054